MIX
Papier aus verantwortungsvollen Quellen
Paper from responsible sources
FSC® C105338

Dr. Priyesh Kanungo

Scheduling in Distributed Computing Environment Using Dynamic Load Balancing

Anchor Academic
Publishing

Kanungo, Priyesh: Scheduling in Distributed Computing Environment Using Dynamic
Load Balancing, Hamburg, Anchor Academic Publishing 2016

Buch-ISBN: 978-3-96067-046-9
PDF-eBook-ISBN: 978-3-96067-546-4
Druck/Herstellung: Anchor Academic Publishing, Hamburg, 2016

Bibliografische Information der Deutschen Nationalbibliothek:
Die Deutsche Nationalbibliothek verzeichnet diese Publikation in der Deutschen
Nationalbibliografie; detaillierte bibliografische Daten sind im Internet über
http://dnb.d-nb.de abrufbar.

Bibliographical Information of the German National Library:
The German National Library lists this publication in the German National Bibliography.
Detailed bibliographic data can be found at: http://dnb.d-nb.de

All rights reserved. This publication may not be reproduced, stored in a retrieval system
or transmitted, in any form or by any means, electronic, mechanical, photocopying,
recording or otherwise, without the prior permission of the publishers.

Das Werk einschließlich aller seiner Teile ist urheberrechtlich geschützt. Jede Verwertung
außerhalb der Grenzen des Urheberrechtsgesetzes ist ohne Zustimmung des Verlages
unzulässig und strafbar. Dies gilt insbesondere für Vervielfältigungen, Übersetzungen,
Mikroverfilmungen und die Einspeicherung und Bearbeitung in elektronischen Systemen.

Die Wiedergabe von Gebrauchsnamen, Handelsnamen, Warenbezeichnungen usw. in
diesem Werk berechtigt auch ohne besondere Kennzeichnung nicht zu der Annahme,
dass solche Namen im Sinne der Warenzeichen- und Markenschutz-Gesetzgebung als frei
zu betrachten wären und daher von jedermann benutzt werden dürften.

Die Informationen in diesem Werk wurden mit Sorgfalt erarbeitet. Dennoch können
Fehler nicht vollständig ausgeschlossen werden und die Diplomica Verlag GmbH, die
Autoren oder Übersetzer übernehmen keine juristische Verantwortung oder irgendeine
Haftung für evtl. verbliebene fehlerhafte Angaben und deren Folgen.

Alle Rechte vorbehalten

© Anchor Academic Publishing, Imprint der Diplomica Verlag GmbH
Hermannstal 119k, 22119 Hamburg
http://www.diplomica-verlag.de, Hamburg 2016
Printed in Germany

SILENT FEATURES OF THIS BOOK

This book illustrates distributed computing concepts and the steps involved in processor management in computing cluster, server cluster and grid. The problem of poor resource utilization due to uneven processing load in distributed systems is studied and techniques of solving the problem using dynamic load balancing have been suggested. It describes detailed algorithms for scheduling using dynamic load balancing. Various theoretical concepts, experiments and examples enable students in understanding the process of dynamic load balancing.

The book is suitable for the students of Distributed Computing, Operating Systems and Advance Operating Systems subjects of B.E., M.C.A., M. Tech. and Ph.D courses.

PREFACE

This century has presented new challenges for distributed systems. These challenges include manifold increase in the number of information sources and the number of users. With the growing demand of resource intensive distributed computing applications, the need of using sophisticated techniques to improve the performance has also increased. Distributed systems suffer from uneven process arrivals which causes load imbalance, where some nodes are overloaded while other nodes are underloaded, or even idle. Dynamic load balancing is a distributed scheduling technique which may be used to improve reliability and overall throughput not only on a cluster of nodes and workstations, but also on a server cluster. It distributes processing workload evenly to improve response time and to maximize resource utilization.

In this book, the problem of poor resource utilization due to uneven processing load in distributed systems is studied and techniques of solving the problem using dynamic load balancing have been suggested. We have addressed the issue of dynamic load balancing in terms of large amount of status information and heavy network traffic. We have presented algorithmic infrastructure for load balancing in a cluster of nodes and workstations as well as a server cluster. Various load indices for load measurement and parameters for performance measurement in a distributed system have been explored. Performances of various load balancing algorithms have been compared using these load indices and parameters. The impacts of load balancing on individual hosts and servers as well as the factors affecting load balancing performance are investigated. For achieving dynamic load balancing, we have presented both non-preemptive as well as preemptive process migration methodologies. We have compared two strategies and suggested parameters to calculate process migration cost. Performance studies with respect to web servers have been carried out and techniques for improving performance of a server cluster have been suggested. New challenges favouring further need of dynamic load balancing in Information Technology applications have also been highlighted.

Dynamic load balancing is found to significantly improve mean response time under unbalanced workload conditions. Load balancing is found to be very effective for small as well as large networks. All nodes, even underloaded nodes, are benefited from load balancing. Similarly all types of jobs get better average response time. Many of the above results are likely to be applicable in general to cluster nodes and workstations, network and web servers and even to networking devices like routers. Dynamic load balancing is cost effective, flexible and reliable strategy to support distributed scheduling even without modifying the system kernels or application programs and without deploying costly powerful servers and nodes.

This book is organized into eight chapters that reflect the stages of DLBs. In Chapter1, we have provided a general overview of the field along with introduction to related areas. We have also mentioned the objective of the proposed research work in this chapter. Rest of the thesis is organized as f+ollows:

Chapter 2 describes the process of load balancing in details. A number of load balancing techniques are defined and studied. The process of collecting the current state of the system, identifying underloaded and overloaded nodes, identifying processes to be transferred and mechanism of transferring processes from underloaded nodes to overloaded nodes has been described. The algorithms for selecting destination node have been described and compared. We also describe an overall methodology for carrying out DLB.

Chapter 3 considers an important issue of load estimation and performance measurement of load balancing algorithms. We have explored various parameters to measure load on the nodes in the system and evaluated various load balancing policies. We have also discussed architecture, implementation and performance evaluation of indices and parameters for capturing and distributing the load using DLB technique.

DLB can not be achieved without process migration. In **Chapter 4**, we discuss about this important phase in DLB. We have compared non-preemptive and preemptive migration methods and described framework for process migration. Technique of transferring process address space from source node to destination node has been explored. We have discussed mechanism for calculating process migration cost and presented methodology for process migration.

A critical problem of performance improvement of network and web servers is highlighted in **Chapter 5.** In this chapter, we have studied the method of performance improvement in server cluster with the help of DLB. Web servers are facing the problem of constantly increasing network traffic and diverse load levels. It is not feasible to use a single powerful server. A cluster of replicated servers can be used and clients' requests can be distributed evenly among the servers in this cluster. We have described the problem of server load balancing and compared various load balancing policies for the cluster. The objective is to identify the algorithm that produces good overall performance.

In **Chapter 6**, we have identified new challenges posed by IT application, which are causing overload in the web based applications and necessitate the use of DLB. We have mainly raised the issues of public domain software, information overload, lack of optimization algorithms in routers, heterogeneity of servers and incompatibility problem of servers. Objective of this chapter is to explore the IT domains where the DLB techniques can be effectively implemented. To meet these challenges only few solutions are available and more solutions are possible. These problems can be tackled by the solutions provided in Chapter 2 to Chapter 5. Possible areas of research have also been mentioned.

TABLE OF CONTENTS

CHAPTER 1 INTRODUCTION TO DISTRIBUTED COMPUTING ENVIRONMENT 1

   1.1 PREAMBLE 1

      1.1.1 Processor Allocation 5

      1.1.2 Distributed Shared Memory (DSM) 6

      1.1.3 Naming 7

      1.1.4 Distributed File System (DFS) 8

   1.2 MOTIVATION BEHIND DYNAMIC LOAD BALANCING 9

   1.3 PROCESS OF LOAD BALANCING 12

   1.4 ORGANIZATION OF THE BOOK 13

      1.4.1 Objectives 13

      1.4.2 Scope 15

CHAPTER 2 DYNAMIC LOAD BALANCING METHODOLOGY 17

   2.1 PREAMBLE 17

   2.2 DYNAMIC LOAD BALANCING METHODOLOGY 19

      2.2.1 Information Policy 19

      2.2.2 Process Transfer 20

      2.2.3 Status Information Exchange 22

      2.2.4 Node Selection 23

      2.2.5 Process Migration 24

2.3 ALGORITHM DESCRIPTION 26

    2.3.1 Informal Description of the Algorithm 26

    2.3.2 Formal Algorithm 29

    2.3.3 Example 30

2.4 SUMMARY 34

CHAPTER 3 LOAD MEASUREMENT AND PERFORMANCE ISSUES IN DLB 35

3.1 PREAMBLE 35

3.2 LOAD INFORMATON MANAGEMENT 36

    3.2.1 Parameters for Static Load Balancing 37

    3.2.2 Processor Queue Length 37

    3.2.3 Execution Time 38

    3.2.4 Process Age 39

3.3 PERFORMANCE MEASUREMENT 41

    3.3.1 Mean Response Time 42

    3.3.2 Processor Utilization 42

    3.3.3 Mean Slow Down 42

3.4 NODE SELECTION TECHNIQUES 43

3.5 ALGORITHM DESCRIPTION 43

    3.5.1 Informal Description of the Algorithm 43

    3.5.2 Formal Algorithm 44

    3.5.3 Example 48

3.6 SUMMARY 51

CHAPTER 4 IMPLEMENTATION OF DYNAMIC LOAD BALANCING THROUGH PROCESS MIGRATION 53

4.1 PREAMBLE 53

4.2 NON-PREEMPTIVE AND PREEMPTIVE MIGRATION 54

4.3 FRAMEWORK FOR PROCESS MIGRATION 57

    4.3.1 Decision to Migrate a Process 57

    4.3.2 Freeze the Process on Source Node 58

    4.3.3 Create an Empty Process on Destination Node 58

    4.3.4 Transfer the Process State 58

    4.3.5 Transfer the Address Space 59

    4.3.6 Forward the Pending Messages 63

    4.3.7 Restart the Process on Destination Node 64

4.4 METHODOLOGY 64

    4.4.1 Informal Description the Algorithm 65

    4.4.2 Formal Algorithm 68

    4.4.3 Example 70

4.5 SUMMARY 73

CHAPTER 5 DYNAMIC LOAD BALANCING IN WEB SERVERS 75

5.1 PREAMBLE 75

5.2 LOAD BALANCING OF CLUSTER SERVER 81

    5.2.1 Random 82

    5.2.2 Round Robin 82

    5.2.3 Weighted Round Robin 82

5.2.4 Shortest Queue 83

5.2.5 Diffusive Load Balancing 84

5.3 LOAD BALANCING METHODOLOGY 86

5.3.1 Informal Description of the Algorithm 86

5.3.2 Formal Algorithm 91

5.3.3 Example 94

5.4 SUMMARY 98

CHAPTER 6   EXPLORING DLB IN INFORMATION TECHNOLOGY 100

6.1 PREAMBLE 100

6.2 RECENT CHALLENGES 102

6.2.1 Public Domain Software 103

6.2.2 Information Overload 104

6.2.3 Mismatch / Incompatibility of Severs 107

6.2.4 Lack of Optimization Algorithm in Routers 108

6.2.5 Performance and Heterogeneity of End Servers 111

6.2.6 Threats and Viruses 112

6.3 SOLUTIONS 114

6.4 FUTURE SCOPE 115

6.5 CONCLUDING REMARKS 117

REFERENCES............... 118

CHAPTER 1

INTRODUCTION TO DISTRIBUTED COMPUTING ENVIRONMENT

1.1 PREAMBLE

Modern operating systems provide access to a large number of resources and facilities including communication and resource sharing. In distributed computing environments, effective scheduling of jobs and efficient resource utilization are critical issues. Hence, there is a great deal of work to be done by an operating system (OS hereafter) as far as scheduling of jobs on various processing elements is concerned. Our thesis addresses this important issue of processor scheduling in a distributed computing environment and emphasizes the need of dynamic load balancing (DLB hereafter) to solve the problem in a cost effective manner.

A conventional OS on a centralized computer manages all the systems' resources viz. processor, memory, devices and information. It provides all the related services like processor allocation, memory management, device management and information management to the users . It may also provide some simple communication services e.g. message passing and file transfer from one computer to other as shown in Fig 1.1.

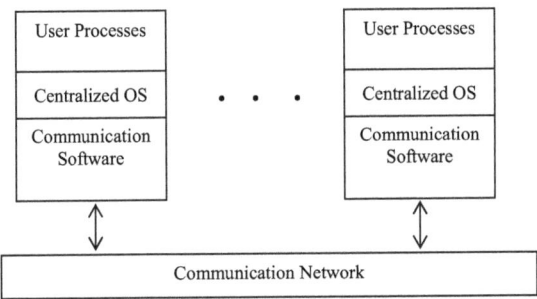

Fig. 1.1: Communication in centralized OS

Network operating system (NOS hereafter) is intended to provide users with global access to resources beyond simple communication available in a centralized system as shown in Fig. 1.2. Major limitation of NOS is that it does not take global control over the resources in the network. The NOS provides access to remote resources by using the facilities and mechanisms supported by local OS. Each computer in the network is managed locally, independent of the other computers. NOS merely provides communication infrastructure to the users. A user must have the knowledge of existence of a remote resource and privileges to access this resource. He must explicitly request NOS to provide connectivity to the remote resource.

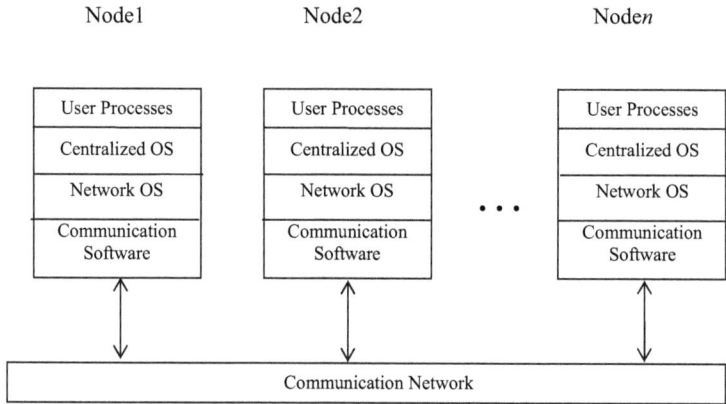

Fig. 1.2: A typical microkernel

Distributed operating system, on the other hand, considers the resources across multiple computer systems (including all resources on all sites) to be globally owned. The system controls and management are based on a single system-wide policy. Contrary to NOS, a distributed operating system is built on a bare machine, not just as an add-on to existing software. The distributed operating system determines the resource requirements of a process and decides how best to execute this process based on best guess or knowledge about the total system as shown in Fig. 1.3.

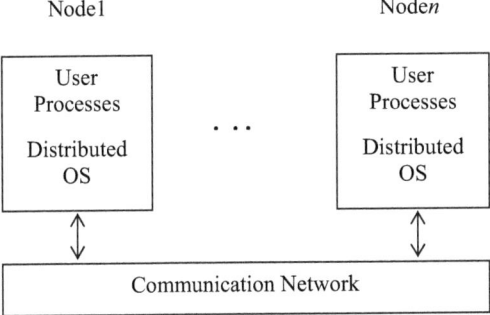

Fig. 1.3: Resource sharing in distributed OS

As the distributed operating system considers various resources available on a computer network to be globally owned, it provides resource sharing in a user transparent way. Thus, it makes the collection of computers to act like a virtual uni-processor system. The system is perceived as a whole and the existence of separate components of the system is concealed from the users and application programmers. A single system-wide policy manages the access to the resources effectively and efficiently. The system determines the processes' resource requirement and allocates the resources in a global way by collecting the information about current status of the total system. In this manner, the functionality of centralized system is made available in managing the resources in a computer network. For a given node, local and remote processes are executed in an identical way [Shiraji,1995].

In the distributed environment, kernel manages only basic resources like processor, memory and inter-process communication (IPC hereafter). It is implemented as microkernel architecture replicated on each node to derive functionality and features of a conventional monolithic kernel. As shown in Fig.1.4, it contains modules for process management, IPC, memory management; interrupt processing, system calls, traps and exceptions. Shared resources and services of the OS are provided by open servers that are implemented above the micro-kernel layer. Local and remote resources are accessed in identical way without the knowledge of their location. DCS are open and scalable. They are capable of detection and recovery of faults. Fault tolerance is achieved with the help of hardware redundancy and software recovery [Petri,1995].

The services provided by the open servers are distributed scheduling, distributed shared memory, distributed file system, name services, remote procedure calls, network servers etc. Apart from the functionality of conventional OS in a centralized environment, a number of other services are provided in a distributed environment as shown in Fig. 1.4.

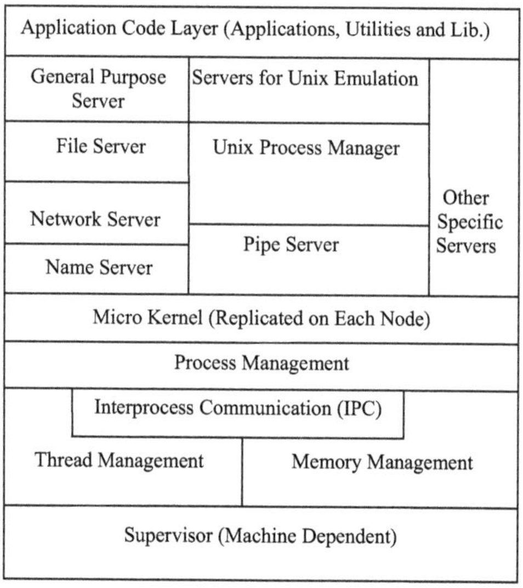

Application Code Layer (Applications, Utilities and Lib.)		
General Purpose Server	Servers for Unix Emulation	
File Server	Unix Process Manager	Other Specific Servers
Network Server	Pipe Server	
Name Server		
Micro Kernel (Replicated on Each Node)		
Process Management		
Interprocess Communication (IPC)		
Thread Management	Memory Management	
Supervisor (Machine Dependent)		

Fig. 1.4: A typical microkernel

The main services provided by distributed operating systems are:

1.1.1 Processor Allocation

Apart from processor scheduling on a specific node, process management tries to make optimal use of processing elements in a distributed environment and provides best possible services to a process by transferring the processes to remote processor, if necessary. Execution of a process is not bounded to local node. How best to execute a process using the resources available in the distributed environment depends on system's best guess about the current state of total system. If the node on which a process is waiting for execution has a long queue, then the process may be shifted to some other node which is either idle or having less number of processes. This ensures proper utilization of resources and improved response time of the process [Alnoso,1988; Ridge,1997].

Main design goals in processor scheduling are better resource utilization, improvement in response time of processes, minimizing network congestion and optimization of scheduling overheads. A number of techniques are used for distributed scheduling of processes. In task assignment approach, a process is treated as a collection of tasks which are scheduled on nodes by taking into consideration the cost of processing each task on every node and IPC cost between each pair of processors. An optimal weight is obtained by finding minimum weight cut-set using network flow algorithm or using heuristics if problem is NP-hard as in case of arbitrary number of processors [Sinha,2001; Barak,1993].

Multithreading can be used for implementing task assignment approach, where each task is organized as a thread. Peer threads can execute concurrently in multiprocessor as well as distributed computing systems (DCS hereafter). A thread is a unit of execution within a process and has its own program counter, register set and stack. However all threads share same address space. Threads also share open files, child processes, semaphores, signals and accounting information. Peer threads do not require protection among them. Threads may be supported at user level or at kernel level. User level threads can be implemented without OS support and allow users to use their own scheduling techniques. Kernel level threads are recognized and supported by the OS. Combination of user level threads and kernel level threads, e.g. scheduler activation or first class threads, provide advantages of both type of threading schemes [Thitikamol,1999].

Load balancing is another technique of distributed scheduling. This approach tries to maximize the resource utilization and throughput by transferring processes from heavily loaded nodes to lightly loaded nodes using some policy. To select a destination node to which a process is to be transferred, load information about the nodes in the system is required. Load sharing approach is different from load balancing which tries to ensure that no node is idle while processes are waiting for execution on some heavily loaded node(s). For transferring a process on the selected node, process's address space is to be moved from source node to the destination node. If the selected process is already executing on the source node, it is to be freezed on source node and restarted on destination node [Rudolf,1991; Baksi,1997].

1.1.2 Distributed Shared Memory (DSM)

Distributed shared memory (DSM hereafter) concept provides large virtual address space by logically combining the physical memory available on different nodes into a single large virtual memory [Stumm,1990; Cybanko,1989]. DSM is implemented in user transparent way so that the system looks like tightly coupled multiprocessor system. A user level server called memory manager performs Page mapping between physical memory of a node and shared virtual memory. If required page is not available in local node's main memory, a page fault causes the page to be transferred from remote node to local node, before resumption of the interrupted instruction. Apart form providing large memory space, DSM provides a high level mechanism for IPC in a loosely coupled system [Ahuja,2005; Stumm,1990]. Figure 1.5 depicts the working of a DSM.

Main design issues in DSM are granularity, structure of memory, memory coherence and data access synchronization. DSM are presently in experimental and prototype stage and research is in progress to make it a viable alternative to message passing systems. DSM can also provide process migration mechanism to support load balancing. This mechanism can be more efficient than a process migration mechanism without DSM. Cost of process migration mechanism using DSM is constant and does not depend on the physical size of process's address space. This mechanism also allows efficient access to all the local and remote files by the migrated process [Vallee,2002].

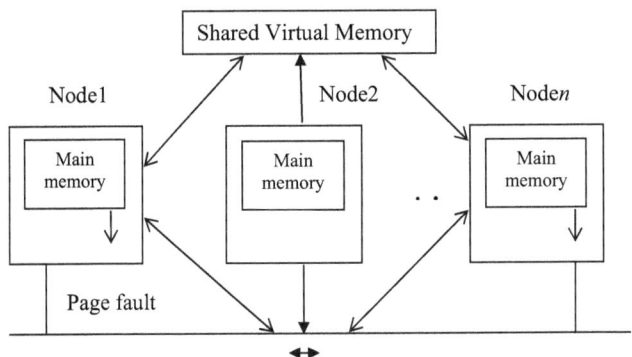

Fig. 1.5: Distributed Shared Memory (DSM)

1.1.3 Naming

Various objects in the DCS like processes, files, nodes, mail boxes and other resources are named and located in the environment by the name server. A name server maintains naming information database and binds object's name to some of its attributes e.g. object location. Name server is a process which maintains information about objects and provides facility to access this information. A specific name server stores the information about a part of object's name in the server. It maps the variable length human oriented names (which are character strings and may not be unique) to fixed length bit patterns called system oriented names. For a client or set of clients, a name agent maintains information about name servers. Therefore to locate an object, the client first contacts the name agent. Name resolution process is used to map the object's name to its location. Several name servers can be used to maintain naming information about objects in the system. A specific server, which stores information about an object, is called its authoritative name server. Protection and sharing of resources to control unauthorized access are implemented through concept of capabilities.

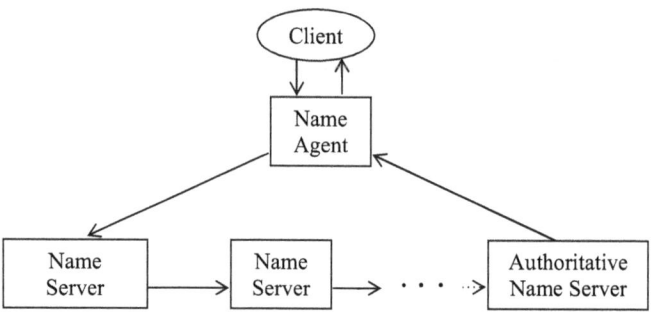

Fig. 1.6: Process of name resolution

Partitioning of name space is the key issue in designing a naming system so that the name space can be distributed over many servers. This distribution of name space is necessary to achieve scalability. Concept of contexts is used for partitioning of name space and a specific context is designated by some clustering condition. Object names are always associated with some particular context. The name resolution algorithm depends on the technique of distributing name space into contexts [Sinha,2001]. The process of name resolution is illustrated with the help of Fig.1.6.

1.1.4 Distributed File System (DFS)

Apart from functionality of a conventional centralized file system like naming, storage, retrieval, sharing and protection, a distributed file system (DFS hereafter) allows users to access remote files and is a basis for naming and print services. Client module of DFS maintains information about network locations, flat file server and directory servers on each node, whereas flat file server implements operation on file data. Operations may be performed at remote server or data caching may be done at client's node. Data caching reduces network delays and results in improved performance of a distributed system. Modifications in the cached data must be propagated back to the file on remote server. File replication is used to increase the reliability, scalability and to reduce network congestion. File replication is also the basis of server clustering and grid computing. Maintaining consistency in replicated copies is an important design issue in DFS [Chen,1995; Wang,1999].

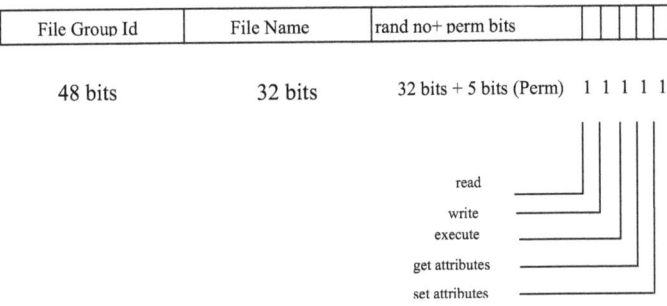

Fig. 1.7: Example of capabilities for a file in DFS

File sharing and protection are achieved through capabilities. Capability is a large integer containing access modes and random number to make guessing almost impracticable. Permissions bits and a random number are encrypted to produce one number. Figure 1.7 shows the example of file capabilities [Coulouris,1994].

1.2 MOTIVATION BEHIND DYNAMIC LOAD BALANCING

This century has been presenting a number of new challenges for large applications that involve communication and coordination with a large number of geographically distributed information resources such as World Wide Web (WWW hereafter). Such applications are supplying information to a large number of geographically dispersed information users [Cardellini,2000]. Our motivation for the research work stems from the profound importance and impact of scheduling and load balancing methods on parallel and distributed systems.

To support such applications, the environment should provide reliable, long term, fault tolerant, highly distributed, heterogeneous and scalable computing with capability of continuous operation. These applications require distributed data collection, large amount of distributed computations, distributed control and distributed output. Such applications are constructed from a variety of computational components like embedded smart sensors, personal digital assistants (PDAs), personal computers, workstations, powerful servers and supercomputers. They may use a large variety of communication media like wires, fiber optic cables and satellite communication with varying degree of link reliability, bandwidth and message loss. The system should be reliable and in case of failures, applications must degrade gracefully. Such applications are expected to have high degree of security and authentication mechanisms.

Such systems can be constructed with the help of new programming environments which integrate computation, data collection, storage, resource management and human computer interface into a communication framework [Kephart,2003; Putrycz,2001; Putrycz,2002]. The framework is expected to provide high availability and reliability through replication of data and computing resource through careful resource management. The network enabled programming environment is based on a number of technologies currently being developed by various sources. Enabled by advanced in hardware, networking infrastructure and advance algorithms, highly compute bound problems in many areas can now be solved successfully using scientific and commercial computing [Casanova,1997].

Scope of distributed applications has grown both in terms of size of network and geographical distance. The rapid growth of computer literacy has led to dramatic size in the number of people using computers and internet applications. This rise has resulted in the development of intense compute-bound resource sharing application. This problem is aggravated with growing complexity of web based applications and services. Network structures and operating environments have become more complex due to growth of e-Commerce and content personalization applications [Garcia,2003]. All these factors together play prominent role in increasing the load across the internet causing severe traffic congestion. DCS are facing constant pressure of increased network traffic and diverse load levels. Performance issues have become more critical due to proliferation of heterogeneous devices, need of authentication and security concerns. Processing load has increased exponentially degrading performance in terms of response time and resource utilization [Cardellini,2002; Ballintijn,2002].

With the growing demand of resource intensive applications, the use of sophisticated techniques to improve the performance has also become necessary. *DLB is one of the distributed scheduling techniques which can be used to improve scalability and overall system throughput in a rapidly growing resource intensive distributed application* [Blumofe,1994]. It is responsible for task scheduling as well as monitoring load variation in the system. In such applications, uneven process arrival may cause load imbalance where some nodes are overloaded while some other nodes are idle. A DLB technique distributes processing workload as evenly as possible among the nodes in a cluster. This helps in improving response time by minimizing job execution time, minimizing communication overheads and maximizing resource utilization. It also tries to preserve fairness in individual job execution. A low priority process, according to a specific scheduling method, should not be overtaken by an arbitrary number of higher priority processes. DLB is realized through process migration. Process migration may be non-preemptive or preemptive. In non-preemptive process migration, processes created on the node of origin are transferred to a selected remote node before execution is started on the source node. On the contrary, in case of preemptive migration, a partially executed task is transferred from an overloaded node to a underloaded node [Kanungo,2006a]. DLB allows cluster of nodes to be used as a cost effective alternative to mainframe computing. It is also used to balance load in a cluster of web servers deployed by websites for processing clients' requests [Berman,1996].

Load balancing technique is crucial for implementing efficient parallel and distributed applications. This technique can be implemented at the application level or at the kernel level. At application level, DLB algorithms adapt themselves to particular characteristics of the underlying parallel and DCS, facilitating the development of portable applications [Devine,1999]. At system level, DLB is of special interest to checkpoint facility and workload estimation [Jiang,2004]. Theoretical results, which can be used as solid foundation for designing efficient and robust scheduling algorithms, are particularly useful for all kinds of systems including clusters and grid [Ditman,2002].

1.3 PROCESS OF LOAD BALANCING

Processor scheduling tries to improve resources utilization and response time of processes in a distributed environment using load balancing. It is not necessary to execute a process on the same node on which it is originated. How best to execute a process using the resources available in the distributed environment depends on system's best guess about the state of total system.

Load balancing can be performed statically or dynamically. Static load balancing is based on information about average system behavior. The selection of processor on which a process is to be executed is based on some predetermined criteria e.g. capabilities of the processors. The algorithms for static load balancing require information about properties of the nodes and process requirements. In DLB technique, the system tries to balance the total system load by transparently transferring the processes from overloaded nodes to underloaded nodes. DLB algorithms collect and respond to systems current state information and are therefore more complex in nature. Their performance is found to be better than static algorithms [Sevcik,1994].

DLB algorithms can be defined by their implementation of policies for load estimation, process transfer, status information exchange, node allocation and process migration. Load estimation policy specifies what workload information is to be collected, when it is to be collected and from where the information is to be gathered. Process transfer policy detects if the load imbalance conditions are prevailing and decides appropriate period of triggering the load balancing operation. State information exchange policy is necessary for exchange of load information among the nodes in the system to identify the nodes, which are either overloaded or underloaded. Polling, broadcasting or on-demand techniques may be used to exchange state information. Broadcasting technique may lead to increased network traffic whereas other techniques allow selected information exchange [Herbsleb,2003]. Node Allocation policy is needed to define the processes on an overloaded source node and to select an underloaded destination node, where these processes will be migrated. Bidding, threshold, shortest or pairing technique may be used to decide a destination node. Process migration technique is required to actually transfer processes from source node to the destination node.

1.4 ORGANIZATION OF THE BOOK

1.4.1 Objectives

In distributed systems, a number of nodes are interconnected to allow resources sharing among the users. Processes arrive at these nodes independently causing variation in load levels on these nodes. Our objective is to explain techniques and methodologies for scheduling the processes among the nodes in the system using DLB. This is necessary for improving resource utilization and providing better response time to the users in a cost effective manner.

The following issues have been explored in this book:

(a) Methodology for DLB: Load balancing policies include transfer policy to determine which node is suitable for participating in load balancing process, selection policy to select processes to be transferred from the sender node, location policy to decide the receiver node where the selected process is to be transferred and information exchange policy to decide what information about current state of the other node(s) is to be collected [Hui,1999; Othaman,2003]. We have addressed the issue of DLB in terms of generating large amount of status information and heavy network traffic and described a comprehensive methodology for DLB.

(b) Effective load indices for measuring workload and parameters for measuring performance of load balancing algorithms: Basic problem associated with DLB algorithms is to identify the indices which are to be used to measure the load on various processors. This load will define the current state of the system. It may not be possible to include all indices in calculating load as this may require exchange of huge amount of information. Effective load index measures will minimize the information about current load in the system, thereby improving the effectiveness of the algorithm. Parameters are also required for measuring performance of load balancing and process migration policies and comparing different algorithms. Various load indices have been investigated for effective load measurement in a computing cluster. We have also described the parameters to measure the performance of DLB algorithms. The objective is to study the effect of different load indices and performance parameters on the performance of DLB algorithms.

(c) Process migration framework for implementing load balancing: DLB can be realized by transferring processes from heavily loaded nodes to lightly loaded nodes which requires process migration. Mechanism of process migration can play important role in DLB. Computation of migration cost is also an important issue. High cost of migration may overrun the benefits achieved from load balancing. Algorithmic infrastructure and methodology for process migration for efficient process migration has been explained.

(d) Load balancing techniques for improving performance of web server cluster: One of the critical a scheduling problems in DCS is to select an effective load distribution scheme for requests arriving on a cluster of replicated servers. Load balancing can be used to improve the performance of server cluster by proper resource utilization and reducing mean response time by distributing workload evenly among servers in the cluster. Our objective is to identify the algorithms that produce good overall system performance. We have investigated the problem of server load balancing and proposed various server load balancing policies.

(e) Exploring DLB to meet the new challenges in Information Technology applications: The need of DLB algorithms in Information Technology applications is increased due to a number new challenges. These challenges have been identified, which contribute to the growth of Internet traffic and have made the use of load balancing necessary in IT applications. Most important ones are: increasing availability of public domain software, lack of optimality in routing algorithms, information overload, performance and heterogeneity of end servers and compatibility problems in servers. We have proposed DLB techniques to meet these challenges.

1.4.2 Scope

This book addresses an important issue of processor scheduling in a distributed computing environment and emphasizes the need of dynamic load balancing to solve the problem in a cost effective manner. Theories, algorithmic framework and methodologies of DLB are described here will be useful in effective utilization of resources and improving response time DCS.

Techniques and methodologies for scheduling the processes may also be useful in balancing uneven workload on a computing cluster effectively. A cluster consists of a number of processing elements as well as storage devices interconnected over a local area network. Clusters are viable alternatives to tightly coupled parallel computers and mainframes due to their ability to offer cost effective environment for running computation intensive parallel applications [Feik,2005]

The book also enables effective workload management in a computational grid. A computational grid consists of a set of interconnected clusters and integrates collaborative use of high performance systems, networks, databases and variety of end user devices that are owned and managed by multiple organizations [Baker,2002]. Major issues in grid computing software include efficient utilization of resources by improved distributed scheduling which fall in the scope of our research work. [Yagobi,2006].

The load balancing methodologies in this book may also be useful in load balancing in a server cluster. In a client/server environment, it is common to have a group of replicated servers which accepts requests from the large number of clients. Clustering of servers enables a transparent growth as physical servers can be added without externally visible network changes [Aron,2000]. The key issue in server load balancing in a DCS is to select an effective load balancing scheme to distribute clients' requests to the servers. The book may help in solving the problem of server load balancing by implementing server load balancing policies.

CHAPTER 2
DYNAMIC LOAD BALANCING METHODOLOGY

2.1 PREAMBLE

In Chapter 1, we mentioned that load balancing is one of the distributed scheduling techniques that try to improve resource utilization and response time of processes in a distributed computing environment by transferring processes from heavily loaded nodes to lightly loaded nodes. In this chapter we describe the DLB methodology.

In a distributed operating system, execution of a process is not bound to a local node. How best to execute a process using the resources available in the distributed environment depends on system's best guess about current state of the total system. If this node is overloaded, processes may be migrated to some other underloaded node. The process of DLB is illustrated by means of Fig.2.1. In this figure, node N1 is overloaded and node N2 is underloaded. Therefore, load balancing is achieved by transferring processes from node N1 to node N2. Here, N3 has only moderate load, therefore, it may not be involved in the process of load balancing. Load balancing may be performed statically or dynamically in a user transparent manner [Alnoso,1988].

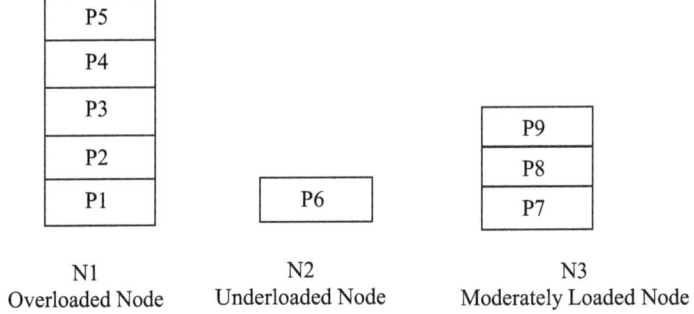

(a) Unbalanced system with nodes N1, N2 and N3

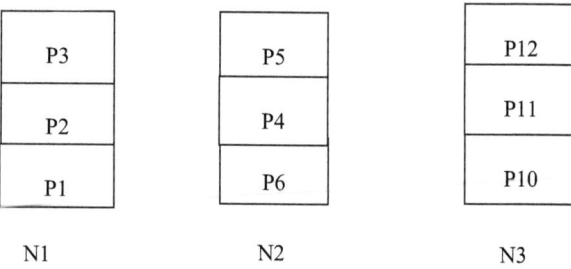

(b) The system after load balancing

Fig. 2.1: The process of load balancing

Static load balancing is based on *apriori* information about average system behavior. Decision regarding the node on which a process is to be executed is made on predetermined basis e.g. capabilities of processors, available memory etc. The algorithm for static load balancing requires information about properties of the nodes and requirements of processes that are to be executed. Decisions related to load balancing are made at compile time when the resource requirement of the processes is estimated. Prior run-time data may also be used for static load balancing. Implementation of static load balancing algorithms is quiet simple as it avoids run-time scheduling overheads. However, a good initial distribution may result in a load imbalance if load characteristics change over time [Bakshi,1997; Zaki,1997].

DLB algorithms collect and respond to system's current state information at run-time without *apriori* knowledge. Their performance is much better than static algorithms as they are able to adjust the short term fluctuations in the overall system load. However DLB algorithms are more complex in nature as they have to collect, store and analyze system's state information continuously. These algorithms may be centralized or distributed. In first case, a centralized server collects current status information of each node. In distributed dynamic scheduling, there are *n* different servers running their processes asynchronously and each server is responsible for scheduling processes of a predetermined set of nodes. These servers may work on cooperative or non-cooperative basis. In cooperative distributed scheduling algorithms, each of these *n* entities cooperates with each other to make decision on the basis of a system-wide objective function. This involves more communication overheads but more stable algorithm resulting in a better performance. There is a trade-off between load balancing and communication cost. If we try to have a perfectly balanced system by exchanging huge amount of load information, heavy network traffic will be generated, resulting in a high communication cost. On the other hand, if we try to minimize the communication overheads, many nodes in the system will be in the unbalanced state.

In Chapter 1, we have highlighted the need of DLB in a distributed computing environment. We now study the methodology used for DLB in details and also suggest a framework for DLB and an algorithm for implementing DLB.

2.2 DYNAMIC LOAD BALANCING METHODOLOGY

In this framework of DLB study, five main steps have been mentioned on which DLB algorithm has been developed. These steps include information policy, process transfer, state information exchange, node allocation and process migration. They are illustrated as under:

2.2.1 Information Policy

Load estimation in DLB is a complex issue. The server must have global knowledge of load on the processors in the system at any instant. Exhaustive approach may not be efficient as it may generate huge amount of network traffic. This will result in increased communication cost. Only selective information needed to achieve an objective function must be gathered. The main concern here is what and how much information about nodes is to be collected [Ferrari,1986]. To measure the load, load indices are required. Some of the following parameters may be used in load balancing:

- Number of processes on a node i.e. processor's queue length. Queue length is the simplest load index.

- Remaining service time required by all the processes on a processor. It is not possible to know how much time a process will require before the process is actually executed, however, we can estimate the remaining time of the processes on the basis of previous computation bursts.
- \Resources required by these processes (e.g. processor time, memory space).
- Nature of applications (compute intensive or I/O intensive process).
- Utilization of processors.
- Architecture of processors (e.g. speed of the processor, shared memory multiprocessors etc.)

2.2.2 Process Transfer

This step involves the decision regarding whether the process originated on a node will be executed locally or on some remote node. A process may be transferred to a remote node if the node of origin is heavily loaded. To select a heavily loaded node, concept of threshold might be used. If the processing load on this node is above threshold, then process will have to be transferred to some underloaded remote node. Threshold level may be computed as:

$$T_i = (C_i \times W_i) / n \qquad (1)$$

where,

C_i is constant depending on processing characteristics of a node i

W_i is workload of node i

n is number of nodes

Threshold value may be single or double. In single threshold value, a node accepts new processes if the workload is below this value. A small change in load (e.g. transfer of just a single process) on the node may change load level of the node from heavily loaded to lightly loaded and vice versa. This leads to excessive process transfer for only marginal improvement in performance. Excessive process transfer is also called processor thrashing and is undesirable activity that results in to poor resource utilization. With double threshold values, the load space is divided into three regions. These regions, as shown in Fig. 2.2 (a), include:

(a) Heavily Loaded region: This region is above *High Threshold Level*.
(b) Moderately Loaded region: This region is below *High Threshold Level* but above *Low Threshold Level*.
(c) Lightly Loaded region: This region is below *Low Threshold Level*.

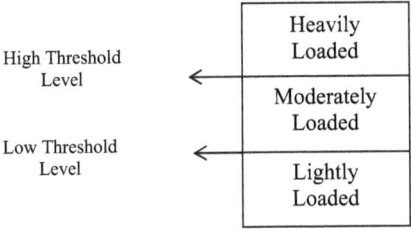

(a) Load regions

PA- Process Arrival
PT- Process Transfer

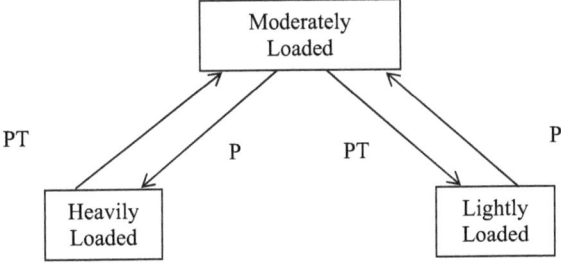

(b) Processor state transition in double threshold

Fig. 2.2: Double threshold level

Processes are migrated to remote node if a node is heavily loaded. A lightly loaded node accepts remote process for execution. In a moderately loaded node, remote processes are not accepted for execution but new processes created on a node are run locally. Double level threshold reduces processor thrashing substantially and results in effective load balancing. Fig. 2.2 (b) illustrates various processor states and their transition from one load region to other.

It is advisable to compute threshold level dynamically rather than using predefined or fixed threshold values as shown in Eq.1. A dynamically calculated threshold value will lead to more effective load balancing in the system [Alnoso,1988].

2.2.3 Status Information Exchange

To select a heavily loaded node or a lightly loaded node among the nodes in the system, status information is to be exchanged dynamically. The exchange of status information may generate heavy network traffic and queuing delays. The techniques are required to keep communication overheads under control. Some of these techniques of information exchange are [Sinha,2001]:

(a) Broadcasting is the simplest technique of information exchange. All the nodes broadcast their load information either periodically or whenever they switch from one load level to another. In case of periodic information exchange, heavy network traffic may be generated resulting in excessive communication costs. We may reduce the information exchange overhead in broadcasting by collecting the information only from those nodes which need to take part in load balancing process, i.e. the nodes which have become either overloaded or underloaded due to change in load level.

(b) Demand Based Exchange ensures that only those nodes receive the load information which want to participate in load balancing i.e. the nodes which are either underloaded or overloaded. On the demand of an underloaded node or an overloaded node, other overloaded or underloaded nodes send their current states to the requesting node. It is obvious that underloaded nodes need information only from overloaded nodes and vice versa. Nodes with same load level need not exchange their status information.

(c) Polling is another technique of information exchange that tries to minimize the network traffic. A node exchanges its load information only when it is expected to do so. The process of information exchange is restricted between two nodes only i.e. a requesting node and the node whose current status has been inquired. The status information transmitted by a node is received only by that node which has requested the load information.

2.2.4 Node Selection

Once a heavily loaded node has been detected and information about the underloaded nodes is collected by the load balancer, a node where the load from current node will be transferred is to be identified. To select a destination node on which a local process would be executed, we use following techniques:

(a) Random Selection: Simplest policy is to transfer the load from existing heavily loaded node to any other randomly selected node. But the problem is that, if the randomly selected destination node is also heavily loaded then eventually a state is reached when the nodes are busy transferring task rather than actually executing them. However, a substantial performance gain has been noticed in case of sender initiated algorithms using random allocation technique [Eager,1986].

(b) Bidding: When a heavily loaded node is searching a destination node for transferring processes, it broadcasts a bid message to other nodes in the system. All eligible nodes quote their best prices depending on resources availability (processor speed, memory size etc). The source node now selects the best quote. The process is then transferred to the selected node provided that the status of destination node is not changed since it submitted its bid. This can be ensured by receiving confirmation from the selected node. Bidding algorithm gives freedom to the nodes in the system whether to participate in the process of load balancing or not. It is not necessary for a lightly loaded node to accept remote processes for execution. Bidding algorithm can be effectively used for load balancing in a heterogeneous system also as the processes can specify their processing needs in their bid messages [Waldspruger,1992].

(c) Probing: In this method, the destination nodes are selected on the basis of their load levels, assuming processes can be transferred from any heavily loaded node to any other lightly loaded node irrespective of exact load on the nodes. Thus, threshold level of the system must be determined before using this algorithm. The overloaded node randomly selects a remote node to see if it is under-loaded. If selected node is not underloaded than another node is tested for underload condition. This process is called probing. Probing continues until an under-loaded node is located. Although probe limit can be fixed to prevent indefinite searching, only a marginal degradation is observed in the speed of the algorithm even after large number of probes [Eager,1986].

(d) Shortest: Shortest technique tries to optimize the load balancing process by selecting a node with minimum load. As the process of determining the least loaded node in the system is complex, the algorithm can be modified by choosing only fixed number of nodes and determining their processing loads. The process of probing can be terminated if some idle node is found. The node with minimum load is selected as underloaded node and processes are transferred there [Wang,1993].

(e) Pairing: This technique tries to minimize the cost of collecting state information which is one of the major problems faced by load balancing algorithms. Any two nodes having large difference between their workloads are paired and load balancing is performed between them. A number of pairs may exist in the system at any instant. However the method has limited load balancing capability, provided the pairs can be changed dynamically [Finkel,1988; Xiao,2000].

2.2.5 Process Migration

Process migration is an important step in realizing DLB. After selecting source node, destination node and the processes to be transferred, the selected processes are to be physically transferred from the source node to the destination node. Migration of processes may be non-preemptive or preemptive. In non-preemptive process migration or process placement, only new processes whose execution is not started on source nodes are transferred. In case of preemptive migration the processes that have started the execution on source node can also be transferred. Before preemptive migration, a running process has to be suspended on the source node, its address space has to be transferred to the destination node and the process has to be restored there. The context block of the process is also transferred and messages meant for the migrating process are to be forwarded to it. If the process migration takes place a number of times then locating the process and redirecting messages to it is a complex activity [Zhu,1997]. Main steps in process migration are being summarized below:

(a) Freezing a process on heavily loaded source node.

(b) Transferring its address space (partially or totally) from source node to the destination node and resuming it on the destination node.

(c) Forwarding messages for migrant process from source node to destination.

(d) Handling communication between migrated process and its coprocesses.

Process migration is complex issue that involves identification of processes on source node which should be migrated for effective load balancing. It has been noticed that if process migration algorithm can identified long processes on heavily loaded nodes and migrate them to underloaded nodes than preemptive migration can give much better results as compared to non-preemptive migration. Preemptive migration results in graceful degradation of the system even if load on the system is excessive. Even the migration of a few large processes can improve performance as a single process on a heavily loaded node degrades the response time of large number of small processes [Harchol-Balter,1997].

Address transfer mechanism also plays an important role in process migration. Even after process migration, the migrant process has residual dependency on the source node e.g. for accessing open files and messages from coprocesses etc. Implementation of process migration may be a complex issue in heterogeneous systems. Calculation of cost of migration is an important factor in deciding the effectiveness of DLB. With the increased communication speed, process migration will become more effective tool for DLB [Richmonds,1997].

2.3 ALGORITHM DESCRIPTION

To illustrate the DLB process in our proposed framework, we describe the algorithm informally as well as formally.

2.3.1 Informal Description of the Algorithm

Algorithm *Dynamic-Load-Balancing* dynamically balances load on the nodes in a computing cluster. Processes arrive randomly on each node with random service time requirements. At each node, processes are executed in FIFO (first in first out) order. Threshold values are calculated at regular intervals as:

$$T = \left(\sum_{i=1}^{n} \sum_{j=1}^{p_i} t_{ij} \right) / n \qquad (2)$$

where,

t_{ij} is the remaining service time of process j on node i

n is the number of nodes

p_i is the number of processes on node i

Load on a node is calculated as the sum of remaining service time of all the processes on a node using formula:

$$W = \sum_{j=1}^{p_i} t_j \qquad (3)$$

where,

    W is workload of a node

    p_i is the number of processes on the node

    t_j is the remaining service time of the process j

The status of each node is checked. If the node is overloaded, its processes are migrated to an underloaded node that has minimum load using *shortest* algorithm. If no underloaded node is found, the processes are executed locally. If a given node is underloaded, it can accept remote processes for execution.

The algorithm also compares the response time of the processes on each node before and after DLB. Response ratio of a process is defined as:

$$R = t / (t + w) \qquad 0 < R <= 1 \qquad (4)$$

where,

    R is the response ratio of the process

    t is service time of the process

    w is missed time

Assumptions made in this algorithm are:

(a) Nodes are homogeneous and communication cost is constant. This will simplify the comparison of results.

(b) Processes are generated randomly on each node. In this algorithm we assume that service time is known in advance. The service time of a process can be estimated using exponential smoothening formula [Finkel,1988]:

$$e_p' = \alpha e_p + (1- \alpha) t \qquad (5)$$

where,

t is service time in most recent stay of process p in short term ready queue. Initial estimates for the first time when the process arrives can be average service time of all the processes

e_p is exponential average of previous arrival in ready queue

e_p' is exponential average of next processor's burst time

α is smoothening factor where $0 \leq \alpha \leq 1$. Higher value of α means less responsive to change in processor burst time

p_i is number of processes on node i

(c) Process migration is non-preemptive i.e. once the execution of a process is started on a node it cannot be migrated to other node.

Load balancer consists of two parts. One module, called server module, collects load information and makes job placements. Another module, called migration module, is responsible for remote execution of the processes. The following steps are involved in the algorithm:

(a) Collect the load information about. Calculate threshold levels.
(b) Identify the overloaded source nodes.
(c) Collect the load information from nodes where processes can be migrated.
(d) Select a destination node.
(e) Select the processes on source node which are suitable for migration. Transfer the processes.

2.3.2 Formal Algorithm

The algorithm *Dynamic-Load-Balancing* are formally described as under:

Algorithm *Dynamic-Load-Balancing*

/* Algorithm for DLB in distributed computing system using process placement*/

{

for each node P in the system

    store its *ready-queue, fptr, rptr, number-of-processes, load-level, mean-response-ratio*;

/* load level may be heavily-loaded or lightly-loaded*/

for each process in the system

store its *creation-node, PID, arr-time, ser-time, response-ratio, dep-time;*

/* new processes arrive at Pi randomly with random service time requirement*/

calculate-load (W, P);

while (true) **do**

    compute-threshold(*load-level*);

    for every processor P in the DCS /*at every node concurrently*/

    {

        if $W > T$ then

            P=heavily-loaded

        else

                P= lightly-loaded;

    while (*P* = heavily-loaded) **do**

            {

                choose-destination-node (*dest-node*);

                if (destination-node-found)

                {

                select (*newprocess*);

                migrate-process (*newprocess, P,dest-node*);

                execute (*newprocess, dest-node*);

                }

            }

    }

} **End of Algorithm**

2.3.3 Example

The algorithm was simulated for cluster of ten nodes using above algorithm and compared the execution of processes with and without DLB using artificial workload instead of real workload to carry out the comparisons. Artificial workload was used as it has a greater flexibility compared to real workload and it is easier to reproduce. Equation (1) to Eq. (5) constitute steps in the formal algorithm.. random process arrival and random service time distribution was assumed with a close queuing network model of a DCS with *n* homogeneous processors, each serving its queue and interconnected by high-speed network with negligible communication delays.

Table 2.1 and the graphs in Fig.2.3 compares the execution of processes without and with DLB. The comparison shows that DLB results in balancing of workload on the nodes and improved average response ratio of processes. various techniques to select an underloaded node were also compared using our algorithm. The comparisons are shown by means of Table 2.2 and Fig. 2.4. The comparison shows that *random* method gives result better than no load balancing at all. Static method gives results better results than random allocation but is not as good as polling. Shortest allocation method gives result better than all other methods.

Table 2.1: Computation of response ratio without and with DLB

Processor	Without DLB			With DLB		
	Load	Response Time	Response Ratio	Load	Response Time	Response Ratio
P1	114	179	0.637	122	145	0.841
P2	100	129	0.775	116	131	0.885
P3	95	156	0.609	99	103	0.961
P4	84	171	0.491	102	112	0.911
P5	110	187	0.588	94	100	0.940
P6	82	113	0.726	107	134	0.799
P7	137	222	0.617	111	123	0.902
P8	76	114	0.667	94	106	0.887
P9	118	204	0.578	90	92	0.978
P10	91	126	0.722	72	77	0.935

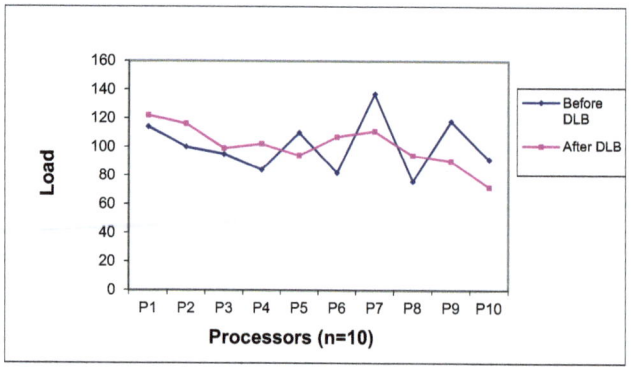

(a) Workload on processors before and after DLB

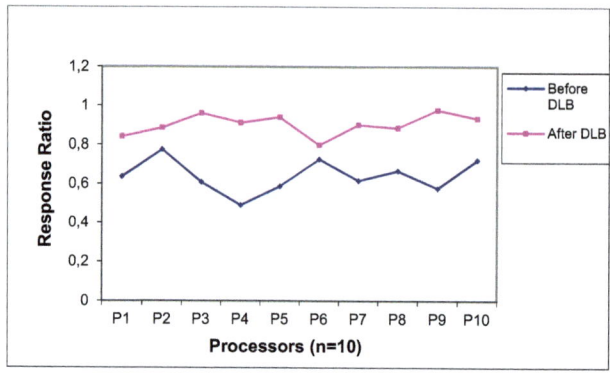

(b) Response ratio on processors before and after DLB

Fig. 2.3: Comparison of workload and response ratio

Table 2.2: Computation of response time for various node selection techniques

	Response Ratio				
Processor	No LB	Static	Random	Probing	Shortest
P6	0.461	0.625	0.593	0.734	0.799
P1	0.523	0.681	0.641	0.752	0.841
P2	0.561	0.712	0.621	0.743	0.885
P8	0.582	0.722	0.701	0.791	0.887
P7	0.617	0.731	0.773	0.821	0.902
P4	0.637	0.773	0.739	0.843	0.911
P10	0.667	0.779	0.833	0.859	0.935
P5	0.722	0.782	0.852	0.881	0.940
P3	0.796	0.820	0.861	0.902	0.961
P9	0.856	0.842	0.881	0.932	0.978

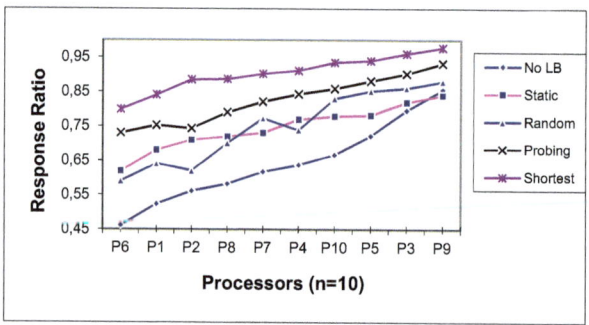

Fig. 2.4: Comparison of node selection techniques (node numbers are in ascending order of response ratio)

2.4 SUMMARY

In this chapter, we have highlighted the problem of constantly increasing pressure of network traffic and diverse load levels in DCS. In distributed applications, performance issues have become more critical due to proliferation of heterogeneous devices, large variety of communication medium and increased security concerns. DLB is a distributed scheduling technique which may be used to improve the performance of DCS. It can be used to ensure effective utilization of processing capabilities on all nodes and improves the response time of the processes in the system by evenly distributing processing load among the nodes.

We have also addressed an issue of DLB in terms of generating large amount of status information and heavy network traffic and suggested the techniques of maintaining current status information in DLB algorithms. The situation of transfer of load from node to node is illustrated by state transition diagram. A comprehensive methodology for DLB is described. Advantages of various DLB techniques are compared and illustrated by means of graphs. Results verify the effectiveness of DLB.

CHAPTER 3
LOAD MEASUREMENT AND PERFORMANCE ISSUES IN DLB

3.1 PREAMBLE

As we have seen in previous chapter, DLB is one of the distributed scheduling techniques, used extensively to improve scalability and overall system throughput in the rapidly growing resource intensive distributed applications. It is responsible for task scheduling as well as monitoring load variation in the system. In such distributed applications, uneven process arrival may cause load imbalance, where some nodes are overloaded while some other nodes are idle. DLB technique distributes processing workload as evenly as possible among the nodes in a cluster. This helps in improving response time by minimizing job's execution time, minimizing communication overheads and maximizing resource utilization. It also tries to preserve fairness in individual job execution so that a low priority process should not be overtaken by an arbitrary number of higher priority processes [Kanungo,2002]. DLB is realized through process migration. DLB allows cluster of nodes to be used as a cost effective alternative to mainframe computing as well as parallel computing [Amiri,2000]. Dynamic load balancing is also used to balance load in a cluster of web servers deployed by websites for processing clients' requests [Abdelzaher,2000]. In present chapter, we have investigated some important issues like measurement of processing workload for taking process transfer decisions and measurement of performance of load balancing algorithms [Petri,1995].

DLB approach can create additional overhead in collecting system state, analyzing the data, making load balancing decisions and transferring the processes from one node to another [Wilson,1998]. Performance of load balancing is closely related to the process information made available to the load balancer, accuracy of the load measurement and the efficiency with which such information is used. Load balancing yields greater performance improvement when workload is heavy and unbalanced. The index used to measure the load in the system strongly affects the performance of load balancing algorithm. It may not be possible to include all load indices in calculating the load, as this requires collecting and exchanging huge amount of information. This may lead to excessive communication cost. Moreover, a poor load index may cause some process migrations which do not contribute to balancing the load in the system, thereby making the situation worse [Dessel,2004].

Therefore, basic problem associated with DLB algorithms is to identify the parameters, which are to be used for estimation of the load on various processors and making load management decisions dynamically. This load will define the current state of the system. Effective load index measures will minimize the communication cost in the system and will allow the load balancer to take quick decisions about load distribution, thereby improving the effectiveness of the algorithm. In a heterogeneous environment, load indices must be adjusted to make them comparable. For example, to compare nodes with different processing powers, their processor utilizations may be divided by respective processing capabilities. Multiple load indices may also be used for making placement decisions. The load index should be easily computable and correlated to those parameters which are to be optimized e.g. response time [Dalhin,2000].

Thus, even though it is established that load balancing facility is necessary for improving the performance of a distributed system, the important issues like load index selection, performance measurement parameters and quality of algorithm needs to be investigated further and are being considered in this chapter.

3.2 LOAD INFORMATON MANAGEMENT

Transfer of processes from overloaded nodes to underloaded nodes requires load balancer to collect load information from the nodes continuously. This helps in identifying overloaded nodes, underloaded nodes and the processes to be transferred. Load information management is therefore a critical issue in DLB. The load balancer must have a global knowledge of load on the nodes in the system at any instant. Although entire state of a node may be transferred, typically only selective information is exchanged to minimize the communication cost. In fact, just a little information may lead to substantial and sometimes, even dramatic performance improvement over no load balancing and perform nearly as well as more complex policies that use large amount of information [Milojicic,2000].

Almost all the load balancing policies require some sort of load indices to measure the workload. Most fundamental issue is the selection of load index to be used in measurement of the load. The choice of load index greatly affects the performance of DLB. We are considering following load indices:

3.2.1 Parameters for Static Load Balancing

In static algorithms, load balancing is performed at the compile time before the start of execution of processes. The following parameter may be used in static load balancing:

(a) Processor parameters including number of processors, speed of processors and ratio of speed of ith processor with respect to a base processor.

(b) The program parameters including data size, number of loop iterations, work per iteration, data communication per iteration and execution time of each iteration on a base processor.

(c) Network parameters including network latency, network bandwidth and network topology.

On the other hand, DLB algorithms collect load information at run time. This information is based on some load index or combination of load indices. Parameters used for load measurement in DLB are being discussed in the following sections.

3.2.2 Processor Queue Length

Number of processes in the ready queue of a node acts as the load measurement index for that node. Using processor queue length, the value of workload can be determined easily. However this index will be effective only if all the processes have nearly same execution time. Using processor queue length, nodes having number of processes more than a threshold value will be overloaded nodes and nodes with number of processes less than the threshold will be the underloaded nodes. The process of load balancing using queue length is illustrated in Fig. 2.2 of Chapter 2.

To decide whether node is overloaded or underloaded, threshold level of the system is computed. Threshold level may be single or double. In single threshold, a node accepts new processed if the workload is below this value. The problem with single threshold value is that even with marginal improvement in performance, excessive process transfer will take place causing processor thrashing. With double threshold level, space is divided into three regions as shown below in Fig. 2.2 (a) of Chapter 2.

Threshold level T is computed as follows:

$$T = \sum_{i=1}^{n} p_i / n \qquad (1)$$

where,

n is the number of nodes in the system.

p_i is the number of processes on node i

In a heterogeneous environment, different nodes may have different processing power. The load is adjusted for processing power of the node.

3.2.3 Execution Time

If the processes have high variation in their execution times, then processor queue length will not be a suitable load index for measurement of processing load. The nodes with less number of processes may high workload due to high service times requirements of the processes in the queue. Therefore, for calculating exact processing load on a node, we have to find sum of execution times of the processes in the queue. But the problem here is regarding estimation of the execution times of the processes. Although the execution time is not known in advance, it can be estimated using some techniques that are based on the time already used by the process. These techniques are:

(a) If the execution pattern of a job is already known, we can find the suitability of a job for transfer. We can also collect the statistics regarding different program types and their average execution times. Based on this statistics, we can identify whether a program type is short or long.

(b) It has been found that processor time, main memory space and I/O requirement of a process can be predicted prior to its execution, using statistical averaging techniques. In the beginning, estimation is made on the basis of identification of the program being executed. We know that a program executes several computation bursts between its creation and termination. On the basis of these computation bursts, predictions are made for weighted mean calculation of resource requirements and actual usage of resource in its most recent stay in the ready queue of the scheduler. This is called exponential smoothening [Devarakonda,1989]. The service time of a process can be estimated using exponential smoothening formula described by equation (5) described in Chapter 2. Using execution time of a process for calculating processing load has only theoretical significance, since it is not possible to estimate precise execution time in advance. However, this technique is suitable for benchmarking to compare the other implementable techniques.

3.2.4 Process Age

Processes that run for longer time are suitable for transfer rather than shorter processes, as the overhead of transferring a short process may override the benefits of load balancing. However input/output intensive jobs, e.g. interactive jobs which heavily access files on the local nodes, are not suitable for migration as the file access cost will be very high on remote nodes. The jobs that are processor bound are suitable for transfer.

Therefore, it is necessary to identify long processes on heavily loaded nodes that have to be transferred. This may be done by keeping track of age of the processes. It has been found that remaining time needed by a process is linearly related to age of the process.

Age refers to the processing time used by the process so far. Workload on a processor is measured by finding the sum of the processing time already used by the processes. Processes longer than the average age of the processes in the system may be long processes.

In addition to using above load indices for load balancing, combination of several load indices into a single index to represent a node's load is an interesting research issues that has to be investigated. More accurate load state information of a node can also be computed by finding average of last few samples of load value on that node. For example:

(a) Last value: This is most simple strategy in which the previous load value from the node is used as its current state information.

(b) Arithmetic mean: Rather than taking the latest load value as current state of the node, arithmetic mean of last three or five most recent load values of that node can be taken as its current load.

(c) Weighted mean: Rather than simply taking arithmetic mean we can take weighted mean of three or five most recent load samples from that node.

In addition to load indices, the performance of load balancing algorithms is also affected by several other factors related to collection of load information. These factors are:

(a) Collection of processing load: Workload can be collected using job traces in trace driven simulation study. Workload can also be generated synthetically. Generally, Poisson's process arrival and exponentially distributed service times are used. Inter-arrival time distribution and service time distribution can also be modeled using Lognormal, Weibull or Pareto distribution if variance in distribution of inter-arrival time and service time is high. In peak times, arrival of processes is less bursty and service time distribution has a low variation.

(b) Load update interval: The collection of load information can be periodic or event based. A typical period is one second or longer while typical events are process creation, termination or migration. The intervals between load index updates should be chosen carefully for the stability of the system. If the interval in collecting load information is too long, the basic objective of load balancing is defeated. This results in poor performance as the load balancer is maintaining outdated information about the system load. On the contrary, collecting load information in short intervals may result in increased networking overheads and over reaction by the load balancing algorithm. [Andreolini,2002].

(c) Load inaccuracy: Accuracy of load information is necessary for making effective decisions in load balancing. Inaccuracy may be caused due to delay in dissemination of information. There is a time delay between measurement of load information and its use. This inaccuracy can be measured as the statistical mean of difference in queue length at arbitrary times t and t+Δt. The inaccuracy increases monotonically with increase in the delay of dissemination of the information.

(d) Load level: Load level is measured as the ratio of mean service time to the mean arrival time as:

Load level = mean service time / mean arrival time   (2)

Load level is called moderate if it is around 50%. In this case inaccuracy is only moderate even if delay is high. Load level is said to be very busy if it is around 90%. In this case load index inaccuracy in more meaningful as it can cause high error rate in load measurement. Therefore, if nodes are busy, information dissemination delay should be small for transferring the information more accurately [Shen,2002].

3.3 PERFORMANCE MEASUREMENT

Load balancing facility improves the performance of the distributed system. Overall system performance can be measured by the following parameters:

3.3.1 Mean Response Time

Performance of a load balancing algorithm can be measured by the response time. Response time is the time elapsed between start of execution of a process and its completion. To achieve the good response time, processes must be distributed evenly among the nodes using appropriate load balancing technique. Good response time also means that the processes don't have to wait too much in the system.

3.3.2 Processor Utilization

Utilization of processor means the percentage of time for which the node is busy in running processes. This index is useful at lower load conditions as at the higher load conditions, even after maximum utilization of the processor, some of the processes are waiting for execution. These processes can't be taken into account for measuring load.

3.3.3 Mean Slow Down

Sometimes response time or waiting time cannot give correct idea about the suffering of processes, particularly when there is huge variation in their processing times. *Slowdown* or *penalty ratio* can be used to measure proportionate suffering of processes in the system irrespective of whether the process is long or short. *Slowdown* of a process is defined as the ratio of total time spent by the process in the system to the execution time of the process and is defined as:

$$P = (t + w + m) / t \qquad \qquad 3)$$

where,

P is mean slowdown of penalty ratio

t is execution time

w is missed or waiting time of a process in queue

m is migration time

3.4 NODE SELECTION TECHNIQUES

Node selection policies have substantial impact on the performance of load balancing algorithms [Kartza,2003]. Different load balancing techniques may be needed in different situations e.g. different architecture, task size variation etc. Techniques that work well in one distributed system may not obtain the same performance in another system.

Node selection policy is needed to define the processes on an overloaded source node and to select an underloaded destination node, where these processes will be migrated. Bidding, threshold, shortest or pairing technique may be used to decide a destination node. Process migration is required to actually transfer processes from source node to the destination node. Node selection and process migration techniques are discussed in details in Section 3.3.

3.5 ALGORITHM DESCRIPTION

Our objective is to compare various load indices that are used to collect load information in the system. We will compare load balancing using three load indices viz. queue length, process age and execution time. The load balancing technique used here is the shortest algorithm in which process from a heavily loaded node are transferred to a node which is having minimum load.

3.5.1 Informal Description of the Algorithm

We have compared the load indices using three different performance parameters. These parameters are:

Case 1: Using mean response time as the measure of the performance.

Case 2: Using processor utilization as the performance measurement index.

Case 3: Using mean slow down as the performance index.

Steps involved in the algorithm are:

1. Collect the system information: The information about various nodes in the system and list of all processes on the nodes, their arrival time and execution time are collected.

2. Collect load information: Load is calculated on each node in the system.

3. Calculate the threshold value: Calculate threshold value of the system to identify heavily loaded nodes.

4. Identify a heavily loaded node: Identify a source node and processes to be transferred.

5. Choose the destination node: Choose least loaded node in the system using the *shortest* algorithm.

6. Transfer processes to destination node: Transfer processes from heavily loaded node to the selected node.

3.5.2 Formal Algorithm

The algorithm for comparing various load indices and performance parameters is formally described as:

Algorithm *Compare-Load-Indices;* /*Algorithm for comparing load indices in DLB. Following load indices have been compared: 1=No load balancing, 2 = Queue Length, 3=Process Age, 4= Execution Time.*/

{

store *threshold, avg-queue-length, avg-age, avg-exec-time* of the system

for each node *P* in the system

store its *ready-queue, fptr, rptr, load-level, mean-response-time, mean-utilization, mean-slowdown, mean-queue-length, mean-age, mean-exec-time;*

/* load level may be heavily-loaded, moderately-loaded or lightly-loaded*/

for each process in the system

store its *creation-node, PID, arr-time, ser-time, response-ratio, dep-time;*

/* *new processes arrive at Pi* */

CreateProcessorQueue (struct processes ());

while (true) **do**

    compute-threshold (T);

for every processor P in the DCS   /*at every node concurrently*/

{

    calculate-load (W, P);

    if $W > T$ then

        load-level=heavily-loaded;

  else

        load-level= lightly-loaded;

```
            while (P = heavily-loaded) do
                {
                        choose-shortest-dest-node(dest-node);
                        if (destination-node-found)
                        {
                                select (newprocess);
                                migrate-process (newprocess, P,dest-node);
                                execute (newprocess, dest-node);
                        }
                }
        }
}
calculate-load (W, P)
{
        if load-index = qlength
                W = sum of queue lengths on processor;
        if load-index is process-age
                W = sum of age of processes on processor queue;
        if load-index is execution-time
                W = sum of execution times of processes on processor queue;
```

}

compute-threshold (*load-level*);

{

    if *load-index* = *qlength*

{

        T = *avg-queue-length* of processors;

}

    if *load-index* = *process-age*

{

        T = *avg-age* of the processes;

}

    if *load-index*=exec-time

    {

        T = *avg-exec-time* of the processes;

    }

} **End of Algorithm**

Assumptions in the algorithm:

(a) The system consists of fixed number of non dedicated nodes with heterogeneous architecture.

(b) Fluctuations in bandwidth are negligible and communication delays are constant.

(c) Algorithm used for load balancing is *shortest*.

(d) Process transfer cost is proportional to the size of the process.

3.5.3 Example

The algorithm we have was simulated for a cluster of eight nodes and compared the load indices using artificial workload to carry out comparisons. Artificial workload provides greater flexibility as compared to real workload and can be easily reproduced. Random process arrival and random service time distribution was assumed. The load balancer consists of two parts. One module called server module that collects load information and makes job placements. Another module called migration module is responsible for remote execution of processes. Table 3.1 through Table 3.3 and Fig. 3.1 through Fig. 3.3 compare the results of simulation studies.

Table 3.1: Computation of mean response time using different load indices

Node Id.	Mean Response Time of Processes			
	Without DLB	Queue Length	Process Age	Exec. Time
3	11	15	18	21
5	18	19	21	20
4	22	23	21	21
7	27	26	23	21
8	32	29	27	23
6	40	32	29	25
2	48	35	32	28
1	59	40	35	30

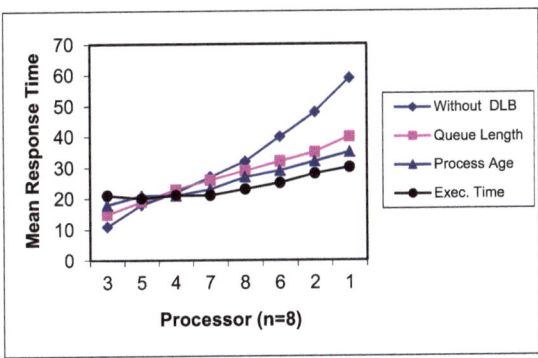

Fig. 3.1: Comparison of mean response time using different load indices (node numbers are in the ascending order of mean response time)

Table 3.2: Computation of processor utilization using different load indices

Node Id.	Utilization of Processors			
	Without DLB	Queue Length	Process Age	Exec. Time
3	35	56	68	79
5	42	61	70	82
4	51	65	71	83
7	59	69	77	87
8	65	74	81	89
6	71	77	83	90
2	79	83	87	92
1	95	85	89	93

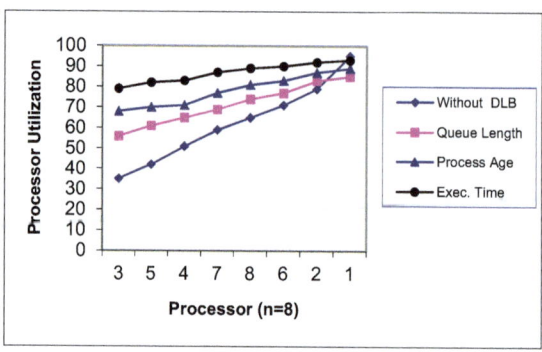

Fig. 3.2: Comparison of processor utilization using different load indices (node numbers are in ascending order of mean response time)

Table 3.3: Computation of mean slowdown using different load indices

Node Id	Mean Slowdown Time of Processes			
	Without DLB	Queue Length	Process Age	Exec. Time
3	1.4	1.6	1.7	1.9
5	1.6	1.7	1.9	1.95
4	2.0	2.1	2.0	2.1
7	2.3	2.4	2.3	2.3
8	2.7	2.9	2.5	2.4
6	3.8	3.1	2.9	2.6
2	4.2	3.5	3.1	2.7
1	5.6	3.8	3.3	2.8

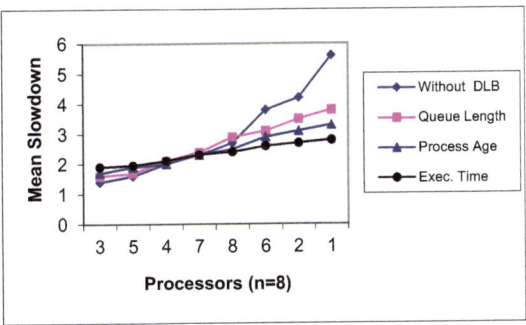

Fig. 3.3: Comparison of mean slowdown different load indices (node numbers are in the ascending order of mean response time)

The graph in Fig. 3.1 compares the three load indices on the basis of mean response time of the processes. Figure 3.2 compares the different load indices on the basis of processor utilization on different nodes. Figure 3.3 compares the load indices on the basis of mean slowdown of the processes in the system. These graphs show that DLB using any of the load indices is better than no load balancing at all. Among the three load indices, execution time as a load index gives better results. But it is difficult to estimate execution time of the processes before actually executing them. However, it works as standard to compare other implementable algorithms. Process age as load indices gives better results than queue length.

3.6 SUMMARY

With the growing demand of resource intensive distributed computing applications, the need of using sophisticated performance improvement techniques has also increased. DLB is one of the techniques used extensively to improve scalability and overall throughput in distributed systems. The fundamental aspect of load balancing in large clusters is that it needs to take into account many different parameters for driving process transfer decisions.

In this chapter, various issues in DLB are investigated and studied various parameters for effective load measurement in a computing cluster. Various indices used to measure the load on the nodes are compared. Comparison is done using different performance parameters. Results obtained are from simulation test instead of measurement from real system. The objective of the simulation was to study the effect of different load indices and performance parameters on the performance of the DLB algorithms.

CHAPTER 4
IMPLEMENTATION OF DYNAMIC LOAD BALANCING THROUGH PROCESS MIGRATION

4.1 PREAMBLE

Although the processing power and storage capacity of computers are increasing, the software complexity and hardware requirements are also increasing at much faster rate. This can be attributed to increasing use of e-Commerce, artificial intelligence, data warehousing and knowledge management applications in information technology. In parallel and multiple computing environments, a programmer defines multiple concurrent tasks encapsulating each task into operating system process that runs on different processors. The node where a process will run is decided at the time of its creation. This schedule of process execution can't be changed even if it is not optimal. Process migration technique attempts to improve performance of parallel and distributed processing environment by allowing processes to move from one node to another to adjust system load as and when it varies greatly on different nodes [Nuttall,1994, Rudolf,1991; Sevcik,1994]. In the present chapter, we discuss about process migration which is an important phase in DLB. We have compared non-preemptive and preemptive migration methods and suggested framework for process migration. Technique of transferring process address space from source node to destination node has been explored. We have suggested mechanism for calculating process migration cost and presented methodology for process migration.

A distributed computing system uses a clustering approach. A cluster is a group of interconnected autonomous computers which are working together as a unified system. Each cluster acts like a virtual uniprocessor system, managed transparently by DCS software. In a cluster, powerful low cost personal computers are combined using high speed ethernet connections to build high performance cluster computing environment with much cheaper price than the expensive parallel machines Clusters are alternative to symmetric multiprocessing to provide high performance and high availability [Perti,2002; Stalling,2003].

Process migration is performed among the computers in a computing cluster. At any instant, many workstations are under-utilized and the processes waiting on busy nodes can exploit their processing power. With the increasing use of internet and WWW applications, possibilities of using process migration also exists in wide area networks as it helps in effective resource utilization in a transparent way. As the distributed computing system allocates the resources on global basis, execution of processes is not restricted to the node of origin and the processes may be shifted from a overloaded node to under-loaded node. This not only improves resource utilization but also provides better response to the processes. Main advantages of process migration include load balancing on cluster of nodes, sharing of resource like memory and hardware devices, detached operations, fault tolerance, improved system management and automatic reconfiguration of servers [Milojicic,2000; Zhang,2005].

We have already seen in Chapter 2 that process migration is a crucial step in DLB. It is performed after identification of heavily loaded source node and lightly loaded destination node by the load balancer. An effective process migration scheme is necessary for an efficient DLB mechanism. In this chapter, we will discuss techniques and steps involved in process migration. We will also propose framework and algorithm for process migration. Process migration strategies will also be compared [Wilson,1998].

4.2 NON-PREEMPTIVE AND PREEMPTIVE MIGRATION

There are two options for selecting processes for migration on an overloaded node. Either select only new processes for transfer or select the processes which have started execution on the source node. In the first option, where only new processes can be selected for transfer is called non-preemptive process migration whereas, the second option, in which executing processes may also be transferred, is called preemptive process migration. In non-preemptive process migration, a new process may be executed on a remote node if the origin node is too busy and the process is likely to get a poor response on this node. Information about the execution times of the processes and user's preference of migratable processes may be helpful in taking effective migration decisions [Jiang,2004].

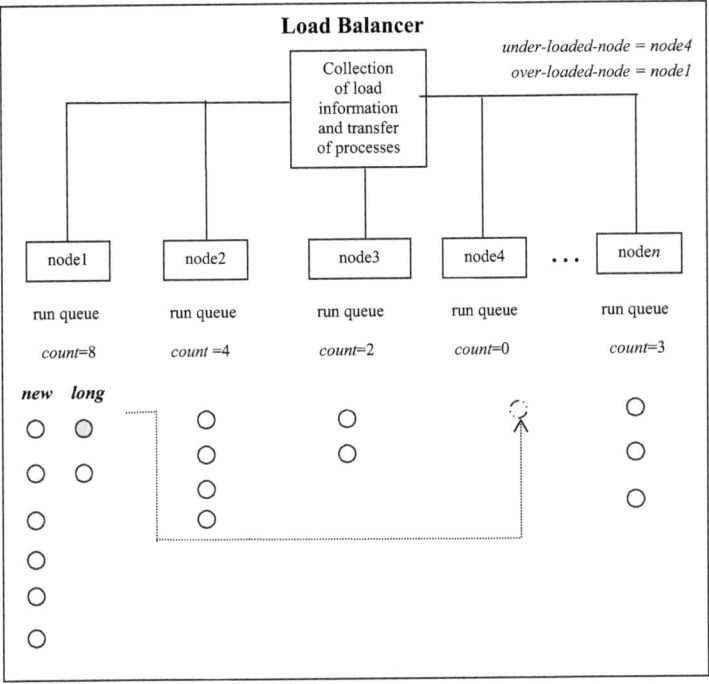

Fig. 4.1: Preemptive process migration

Preemptive process migration refers to migration of a partially executed task as shown in Fig. 4.1. It is usually performed in user transparent manner. Even when the load on the system becomes excessive, degradation in performance of system is graceful [Milojicic,2000]. Although some researchers discourage the use of preemptive migration for load balancing compared to non-preemptive migration [Eager,1988], recent studies based on more realistic workload assumptions show that preemptive migration can be a better option than non-preemptive migration even with high cost of migration. These can be possible due to high-speed networks, increased processing power and improved connectivity among users. Possibility exists to employ DSM concept to make process migration more efficient and reduce migration costs. In DSM, physical memory pages need not be transferred from one node to another. Only high level information about memory and files accessed by the system need be transferred. Therefore, size of information to be transferred is constant and does not depend on the address space of the processes. In this manner, migration cost remains under control. DSM also allows access to open files on its new execution node in the same way as it was doing on its previous execution node [Thitikamol,1999; Vallee,2002].

Selection of the processes for migration depends on many factors like their age, migration cost, load level of the source and destination nodes etc. Migration of small processes will not be much effective as their migration cost will be comparable to their execution time. Processes with long remaining lifetime should be selected for migration. If the migration of a process is cheaper than its execution cost, it is likely to be migrated. Therefore, one of the important tasks in process migration algorithms is identification for small and long processes for taking migration decisions. However, in case of high-speed networks and improved connectivity among nodes, migration of small processes can also be beneficial [Harchol-Balter,1997; Wang,1993].

Preemptive process migration is further complicated if two machines are architecturally different or have different operating systems. In case of heterogeneous distributed environment, process migration mechanism poses a number of problems, e.g. mechanism to migrate execution state, mechanism to migrate memory state and mechanism to communication state of a process. Transfer of execution state is machine dependent. For transferring memory state, problem arises due to different memory configuration and memory management schemes among architecturally different computers. Memory on different machines can have different addressing modes and data formats. Facility for migration of communication state of processes has to be carefully designed for minimizing overheads. In case of heterogeneous computers, the data must be translated from source computer format to destination computer's format. External data representation mechanism can also be used for simplifying process migration. Such a external data representation format must provide capability of different data representations e.g. characters, integers and floating point numbers. Process state has to be saved in machine dependent form. In recent systems, heterogeneity can be also handled at language level e.g. byte code representation in Java. In architecturally different machines, application programs should cooperate with migration software for successful migration so the migration is no longer transparent to the users [Hu,1998].

Process migration may be implemented at user level or at the kernel level. In user level process migration, a modified system library intercepts the system call. The application to be migrated should be linked with this library. User level implementation has better portability but it is slower as compared to kernel level implementation. As user level migration is not transparent to the users, it is not suited to DLB applications. However it may be useful for supporting long running applications. If the migration is supported by kernel, the existing programs run without modifications or relinking. Kernel level migration is faster and transparent as compared to user level migration. However, modifying the kernel to support migration is more complex as compared to developing user level software to support migration. Extensible kernels may use alternative approach by allowing user implemented migration modules to be included in kernel. They have to provide facility of extracting process state from the operating system [Milojicic,2000].

4.3 FRAMEWORK FOR PROCESS MIGRATION

In this section, description of an infrastructure for preemptive process migration is present. Steps involved in process migration are being discussed in the following sub-sections.

4.3.1 Decision to Migrate a Process

Keep track of the current system load and take decision regarding process migration i.e. the processes to be migrated, the heavily loaded source node and the lightly loaded destination node. As seen in Chapter 3, an information management policy used in load balancer keeps track of the system load using some load indices e.g. processor queue length, estimated execution time of the processes etc. Overloaded nodes and underloaded nodes are identified on the basis of threshold level. Decision to transfer the process on a heavily loaded node is based on estimated remaining execution time of the processes. As some communication overheads are associated with process migration, selection of long process rather than short processes can result in improving the efficiency of process migration mechanism [Selvam,2001].

4.3.2 Freeze the Process on Source Node

Remove a ready process from ready queue and block it. The process state is to be extracted from the operating system kernel. The process state consists of address space, list of open file, processor register state and process stack. If the process is executing a system call and sleeping at uninterruptible priority, then the blocking is to be delayed till the system call is complete. Process may also have to wait for completion of fast I/O operations like disk I/O. Store the messages for migrating processes on its message queue. Access to open files by the process after migration is complex issue, as it has residual dependency on the source node.

4.3.3 Create an Empty Process on Destination Node

Send the messages regarding size and location of the process to be migrated to the destination kernel. Kernel creates an empty process and reserves memory space for the migrating process. The migrated state of the process will be stored in this empty process on the destination node. However, the execution of the process on destination node is to be resumed depending on the address transfer mechanism used in the algorithm.

4.3.4 Transfer the Process State

Process state includes program counters, register states, status of open files (I/O queues and buffers), resource usage, capabilities, dispatch information, memory tables, process links etc. The important issue here is how much state is to be migrated. The transferred process state is stored in the empty copy of the process created in Step 3 above.

4.3.5 Transfer the Address Space

Copy the address space including program text, data and stack into destination process. One of the following methods may be used to transfer the execution state and address space of the process [Richmonds,1997]:

(a) Eager-Copy: Transfer the execution state and entire address space of the migrating process before its execution is started on the destination node as shown in Fig. 4.2. This is also called total freezing. Although, this mechanism is simple, the time between freezing the process on source node and resuming it on destination node is longer, resulting in high migration cost.

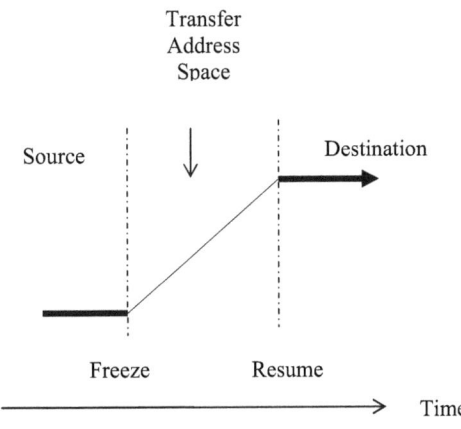

Fig. 4.2: Eager-Copy

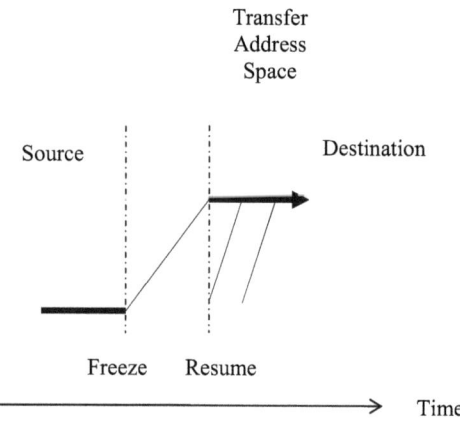

Fig. 4.3: Lazy-Copy

(b) Lazy-Copy: Transfer the minimum necessary information for the process to resume its execution on the destination node. This may include part of kernel data structure and a small part of address space, say the current working set of the process. Other information is transferred on demand as shown in Fig.4.3. This mechanism works in the similar way as demand paging memory management algorithm used in a conventional operating system. Although, this mechanism has minimum delay between decision to migrate the process and resumption of its execution on the destination node, the process continues to be dependent on the source node, thereby adding to runtime cost of the process. Paging support is also necessary for using this technique. Therefore, it is desirable to have high-speed data transfer and less network latency.

(c) Pre-Copy: Don't suspend migrating process on source computer until most of the address space is copied to destination process. Transfer the dirty pages only after the process has been suspended on the source node as shown in Fig 4.4. Freezing time in Pre-Copy is much less, as in case of Lazy-Copy, but a new process has to be created on destination to transfer address space while the migrating process is executing on source node.

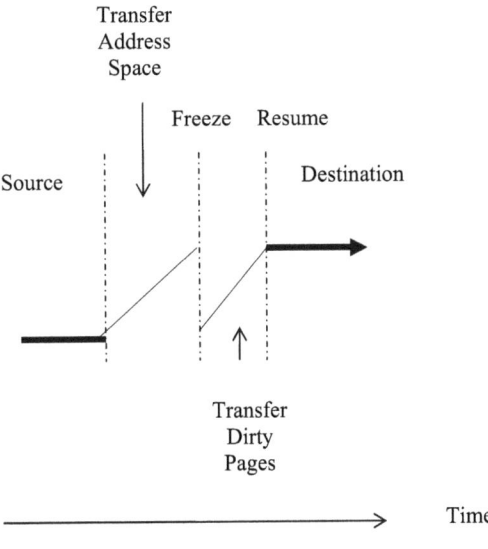

Fig. 4.4: Pre-Copy

The operating systems on both source as well as destination node must support demand paging technique. In this technique, runtime overheads are much less as compared to Lazy-Copy.

(d) Flushing: Suspended the process on the source node and flush the dirty pages to a file server. The migrated process has no residual dependency on source node for address space but now the process is dependent on a network file server which is used to support virtual memory as backing store and can be accessed from anywhere in the network. Such a scheme has to be supported by efficient processing of page faults. Figure 4.5 shows the transfer of process address space using flushing method. This technique is a modification of Pre-Copy scheme mentioned above.

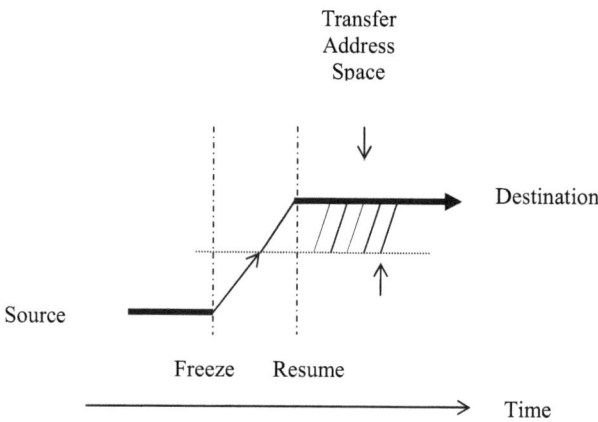

Fig. 4.5: Flushing

(e) Post-Copy: After the minimum pages are transferred from source node to the destination, resume its execution on destination as soon as possible. Transfer the remaining state information and address space parallel to this execution is as shown in Fig. 4.6. If after the start of execution, process requires data not available on destination, send request to the host. Like lazy-Copy, the delay between the decision to migrate the process and resumption of its execution is short, but unlike Lazy-Copy, process does not have any dependency on source node after the process is migrated [Richmonds,1997].

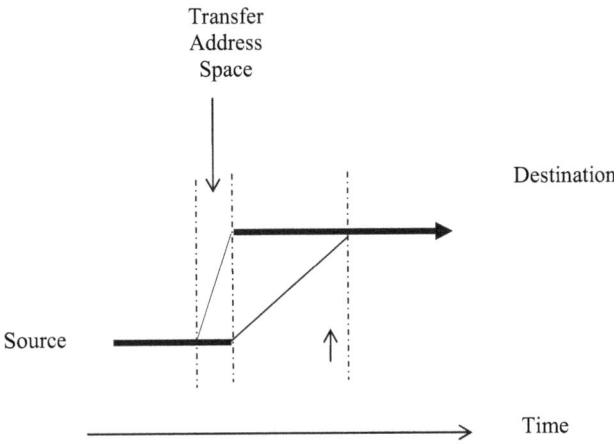

Fig. 4.6: Post-Copy

4.3.6 Forward the Pending Messages

Process migration facility must ensure that all messages meant for the migrated process which it could not receive due to freezing and migration to the destination node, eventually reach to the process. Such messages may include:

(a) Pending messages: Messages queued at the source node when process is freezed but not resumed on destination node. Such messages are waiting for the process to receive them. These messages are to be forwarded to the destination node when the process reaches there.

(b) In route messages: Messages received at source node after the process started execution on the destination node. These messages must be forwarded immediately to the process on the destination node, the address of which is available at the source node. If the system is supporting multiple migrations of a process, the process might have been re-migrated from destination node to some other node and its address is not known to the previous source node. In such cases, migration system must use a mechanism for keeping track of resending the message to the current location of the process.

(c) Future messages: As the processes which want to send messages to the migrated process know its address, messages is sent directly to the migrated process on destination node itself. As in case of (b) above, if the migration system supports multiple migrations, then a mechanism should be evolved to keep track current location of the migrated process.

4.3.7 Restart the Process on Destination Node

Once the minimum state necessary for resuming the execution of the process is transferred, the process resumes its execution on the destination node. The process can now start receiving messages meant for it. The new address of this process must be communicated to the rest of processes in the system by means of link from the previous location or through a broadcasting mechanism.

4.4 METHODOLOGY

To illustrate the preemptive process migration in the proposed framework, the algorithm is describe informally as well as formally. In non-preemptive migration, the algorithm selects new processes. In case of preemptive migration, algorithm selects a process running for the longest period of time on a heavily loaded node. Following assumptions have been made in the algorithm:

(a) Fluctuations in the network bandwidth are negligible.

(b) Migration cost is proportional to the physical size of the process to be migrated.

(c) Communication delays are constant.

(d) Penalty ratio cannot be less than 1 and utilization of processor can not be more than 100%.

4.4.1 Informal Description the Algorithm

A centralized load balancer performs migration by selecting heavily loaded nodes. Load is measured on the basis of ready queue length. The node having number of processes greater than upper threshold is a heavily loaded source node and the node with smallest number of processes is called lightly loaded destination node. In case of tie, the node with higher utilization factor is a heavily loaded source node and a node with lower utilization factor is the lightly loaded destination node [Zhu,1997].

Threshold is computed as follows:

$$T = \left(\sum_{i=1}^{n} p_i \right) / n \qquad (1)$$

Where,

T is the threshold level

n is the number of nodes in the system

p_i is the number of processes on node i

For migration, processes with age greater than the average lifetime of processes on that node are selected. These processes will be processor bound processes. Average lifetime of processes on a node i is:

$$L_A = \left(\sum_{j=1}^{p_i} L_j \right) / p_i \qquad (2)$$

Where,

L_A is average lifetime of processes on a node

L_j is lifetime of a process j

Age of a process refers to processor time used by the process so far. Two queues are maintained to store ready processes. The *new* queue will contain new process in the ready queue. In *long* queue, long processes having age more than average age of processes will be stored on a heavily loaded processor. Communication cost for non-preemptive migration is computed as:

$$C = \sum C_{ij} \qquad (3)$$

Where,

C_{ij} is the cost of communication from node *i* to node *j*. We assume that the cost of traversing each link is 1

For preemptive migration, communication cost C is:

$$C = C_{ij} + C_s \qquad (4)$$

Where,

C_s is the state transfer cost

If average communication cost between two nodes *i* and *j* of the system is C_{ijavg}, then for a process to be eligible for migration, its communication cost is less than H times average communication cost as follows:

$$C_{max} <= H * C_{ijavg} \qquad (5)$$

Where,

> H is the number of hops between source and destination nodes
>
> A process can be migrated only if migration eligibility flag M is set to 1
>
> Penalty ratio P of a process is the ratio of total time spent by the process in the system to execution time of the process and is computed as described equation (3) in Chapter 3:

Memory transfer cost is an important criterion for preemptive migration. The performance of preemptive migration is poor if cost of migration cost increases. When the memory transfer cost is too high, it is difficult to find a process suitable for migration. Although we have not considered size of the process in calculation of migration cost, it may also be included. For transferring entire address space (Eager-Copy), the cost is:

$$mcost = F + S/B \qquad (6)$$

Where,

> $mcost$ is the memory transfer cost
>
> F is time required to transfer a null process (fixed cost)
>
> B is bandwidth
>
> S is size of the process

For lazy transfer in paging systems, where it is not necessary to transfer entire address space of the process, the pages may be migrated on demand. Cost may be computed as follows:

$$mcost = F + pages*pcost \qquad (7)$$

Where,

> *pages* is the number of pages demanded at the destination node
>
> *pcost* is the cost of transferring one page

The Equation (1) to Eq. (7) given above and Eq. (3) given in Chapter 3 constitute the steps in the formal algorithm.

4.4.2 Formal Algorithm

The algorithm for process migration is formally described as under:

Algorithm *Process-Migration*

/*Algorithm for process migration in a distributed computing system. Migration policies are: 0 = no migration, 1 = non-preemptive migration and 2 = preemptive migration of processes with age greater than average age of processes on heavily loaded nodes*/

{

for each *node*, store the processes arrived in the

queue, fptr, rptr, number-of-processes, load-level, mean-penalty-ratio, utilization;

/*load-level of a node may be heavily loaded or lightly loaded/*

for each process P_i in the system, store its

creation-node, PID, arr-time, ser-time, penalty-ratio, and dep-time

{

new processes arrive at P_i randomly with

random service time requirement;

calculate-load (W_i, P_i);

calculate-average-age(LA, Pi);

while (true) **do**

    compute-threshold;

    for every processor P_i in the DCS   /* at every node concurrently*/

    {

if $Wi > T$ **then**

    P_i =heavily-loaded;

else

    P_i =lightly-loaded;

    while (P_i = heavily-loaded)

    {

        choose-destination-node( );

        if (destination-node-found)

        case1: process-placement ;

            select (*newprocess*);

            migrate(*newprocess, source, destination*);

            execute(*newprocess, destination*)

       case2: preemptive-migration select *(process)*;

  migrate(*newprocess, source ,destination*);

  execute(*process, destination*);

        }

      }

    }

  }

End of Algorithm

4.4.3 Example

Using Equation (1) to Eq. (7) in Section 4.4.1 and Eq. (3) in Section 4.3.3, non-preemptive and preemptive migration implemented. using artificial workload instead of real workload to carry out the comparisons. Artificial workload has been chosen as it provides greater flexibility as compared to real workloads and it is easier to reproduce. Random process arrival and random service time distribution was assumed. Virtual processors are used to process the workloads. DCS was considere with n homogeneous processors each serving its queue and interconnected by high-speed network with negligible communication delays. The system was examined with $n=10$.

Table 4.1: Computation of penalty ratio and utilization by the algorithm

Node	Penalty Ratio			Utilization		
	no-migr	non-preemp	preemp	no-migr	non-preemp	Preemp
N1	3.38	2.77	1.90	100	100	100
N2	1.00	1.13	1.25	30	43	65
N3	5.46	4.25	3.41	100	100	100
N4	1.00	1.05	1.29	22	51	78
N5	1.00	1.00	1.15	21	47	73
N6	4.80	3.72	2.89	100	100	100
N7	1.00	1.12	1.30	24	35	72
N8	3.90	3.11	2.33	100	100	100
N9	1.00	1.13	1.24	34	49	79

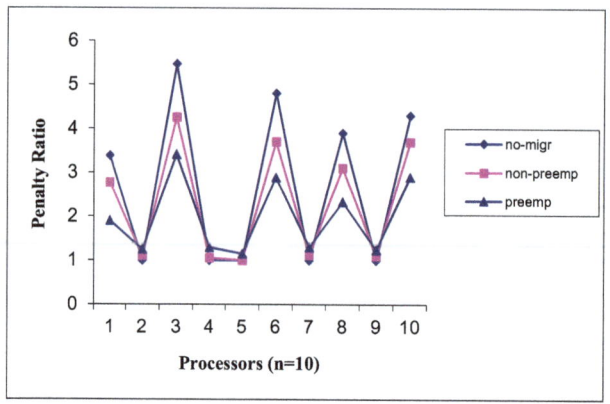

(a) Penalty ratio of processes on individual nodes

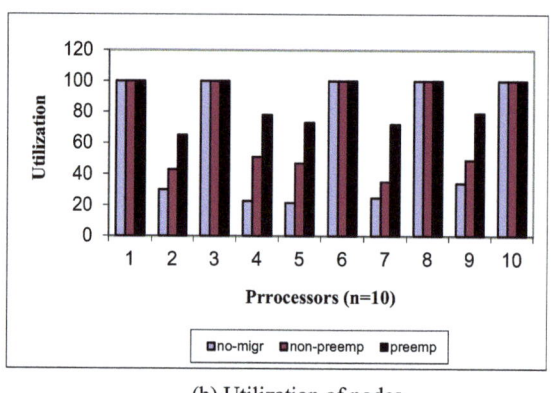

(b) Utilization of nodes

Fig. 4.7: Comparison of non-preemptive and preemptive migration

Load balancer consists of two parts. One module, called *server* module, collects load information and makes job placements. Another module, called *migration* module, is responsible for migrating processes to remote nodes for execution. Following steps are involved in the algorithm:

(a) Collect the load information and compute threshold level.

(b) Identify the overloaded nodes from where processes are to be transferred.

(c) Collect the load information from nodes to which processes can be migrated.

(d) Select a destination node.

(e) Select the processes on source node which are suitable for migration.

>Case I: Select only new processes on the source node.

>Case II: Select executing processes whose lifetime is greater than the average life-time of the processes on the node.

(f) Migrate these processes.

Non-preemptive and preemptive process migration algorithms are compared with the help of an example. Table 4.1 shows the computations by the algorithm. Results are also illustrated by means of graphs in Fig 4.7. Figure 4.7(a) compares their penalty ratio of the processes and Fig. 4.7(b) compares the processor utilization. These graphs reveal the advantages of process migration. Comparison of non-preemptive and preemptive process migration policies shows that preemptive process migration results in improved service to the processes and improved resource utilization as compared to no migration or non-preemptive migration.

4.5 SUMMARY

In this chapter, we have studied process migration, which is a critical issue in DLB. It also finds its application in fault tolerance and improved system management. With the increasing use of web applications and high performance facility-shift from mainframe and supercomputers to distributed computing environment, the issue is gaining more attention in research community. Process migration may be non-preemptive or preemptive. In non-preemptive process migration, processes created on an overloaded node are transferred to selected remote node before their execution starts on the node of origin. On the contrary, a partially executed process can be freezed on an overloaded source node and migrated to some other underloaded node in preemptive migration. Most of the currently available tools do not consider the parameters like load on the processor, network characteristics and memory usage.

The above issue is addressed for achieving effective DLB. Key concepts in process migration are illustrated with the help of diagrams. Suitability of non-preemptive and preemptive process migration for DLB is also investigated. Algorithmic infrastructure for efficient process migration is described. Algorithm for preemptive process migration has been stated. Advantages of preemptive process migration have been illustrated by means of graph. It has been observed that migration of even a few large processes can improve system performance. Just one long process on a heavily loaded node increases the penalty ratio of a number of small processes. With the increased communication speed and as a result of users getting more and more connected on intranet and WWW applications, preemptive process migration has become effective and crucial tool for DLB based on its ability to identify long processes.

CHAPTER 5
DYNAMIC LOAD BALANCING IN WEB SERVERS

5.1 PREAMBLE

In client server environment, clients are usually large in number. Much of the processing work of clients is now being shifted to servers which are primarily used for providing web services. Web servers are the means of interoperating between different software applications running on variety of platforms, operating systems and programming languages [Watts,1998a]. Most of the commercial application servers support web services. Web services are presenting enormous opportunities as well as a number of challenges by fundamentally changing the method of doing business and recasting the vendor customer relationship. More and more businesses are deploying network solutions being used by increasing number of people. With the phenomenal growth of IP traffic due to market expansion, server sites are overwhelmed with processing load. In the coming years, even small companies will have to establish their Internet and Intranet presence to survive. In this chapter, we will study the methods of performance improvement in server cluster with the help of DLB techniques [Menasce,2000].

Although, in recent years, both network and server capacities are improved, web applications are no more used for simple communication and browsing for getting static information. WWW has become the medium of conducting personal and commercial transactions that require dynamic computation and secure communication with large number of servers through the use of middleware and application software. With the increase in heterogeneous client devices and network bandwidth, the use of techniques for improving performance [Nahum,2002] of web server system has become necessary. There are essentially two ways for server sites to manage increased traffic; deploy a more powerful server or add additional servers to a cluster of replicated servers without disrupting service [Cardellini,2002; Garcia,2003; McWherter,2004].

In a client server environment, it is common to have a cluster of replicated servers which accepts requests from the large number of clients. A cluster is a group of servers with identical contents, networked together to act as a single virtual server and capable of growing with the corporate needs. Clustering enables a transparent growth as physical servers can be added without externally visible network changes. Clustering also improves fault tolerance so that a physical server can be taken down for maintenance or repair without network shutdown. A cluster server exhibits high availability and throughput characteristics which are much better than a costly, largest single server [Harchol-Balter,1999; Harchol-Balter,2003]. An example of web cluster is shown in Fig. 5.1. Cluster of servers may have heterogeneous servers. Their configuration and load level may also change dynamically. Clusters may also be integrated into a computational grid.

For a server cluster to achieve its high performance and high availability potential, DLB technique is required. Combining load balancing with cluster of low cost servers is a cost effective, flexible and reliable strategy to support web-based services. Load balancing optimizes request distribution among servers based on factors like server capacity, availability, mean response time, current load, historical performance and administrative weights. It also improves the scalability and overall throughput of the distributed computing system [Abdelzaher,2000;Fu,2003].

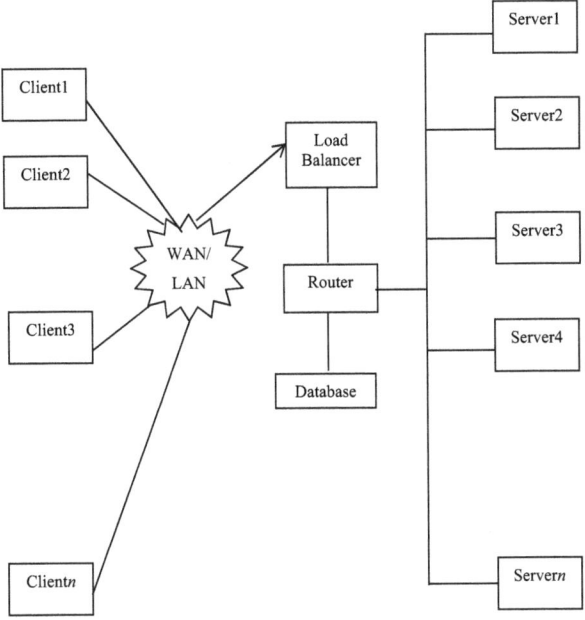

Fig. 5.1: Load balancing in a network of servers

Main advantages of using load balancing in server cluster are:

(a) 24X7 availability with consistent response time and resource availability without failure.

(b) Manageability and monitoring of server cluster to suit different needs and requirements.

(c) Performance improvement by evenly distributing the clients' requests among the servers in the cluster.

(d) Scalability so that more servers can be added or removed from the cluster dynamically in a transparent way.

(e) Cost effectiveness as compared to using a single costly server.

Load balancer sits between internet and the server cluster. It intercepts client requests transparently before they are dispatched to a server. Upon arrival of a request, it takes instantaneous intelligent decision about the server which can best satisfy the request. Thus, the load balancer is a middleware, which distributes client workload equitably among various backend servers in order to obtain the best response time for a workload [Castro,1999; Ghini,2001].

Load balancing may even be supported by admission control mechanism, which controls the rate at which new requests from clients are accepted for processing by the web servers. The requests that may result in bottleneck are not admitted in the cluster system. Admission control should be performed as early as possible, as, by the time the request is rejected, it might have already wasted significant resources. Incorporating admission control in server load balancing scheme reduces processing load of the servers and further improves their performance. This ensures that accepted requests receive a good response [Chen,2001; Iyer,2000]. Admission control mechanism uses various performance measures of the servers, for example, server queue length, server utilization factor, memory consumption etc. for accepting or rejecting clients' requests. For this purpose servers' performance levels has to be periodically monitored [Aweya,2002]. Load balancing mechanism distributes the incoming requests across the web servers in the cluster in proportion to their capacity [Othama,2001; Othama,2003]. Steps in balancing load on server cluster are shown in Fig. 5.2. These steps include:

(a) The client sends a request which is intercepted by the load balancer transparently.

(b) The load balancer collects the state of the servers.

(c) The load balancer selects an underloaded server.

(d) The load balancer redirects the client's request to the newly selected server.

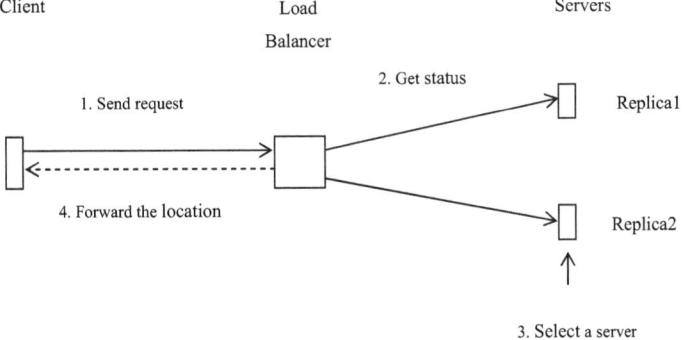

Fig. 5.2: Steps in server load balancing

Load balancing algorithms may be state blind or state aware. In state blind policies, the dispatcher assigns requests to servers using static information. No dynamic information is used. *Random* and *round robin* are the state blind policies. In *random* allocation, the incoming requests are distributed uniformly to the server nodes with equal probability of reaching any server. *Round robin* method uses a circular list and pointer to last entry for making dispatch decisions. Modern day clusters are being developed with heterogeneous computers, a number of interaction devices and variety of communication medium. Randomized load distribution schemes may not be sufficient. The load balancing system should be able to support a heterogeneous system of servers whose configuration may vary frequently. Configuration may change as a result of addition or removal of servers, server breakdown problem or link failure. *Weighted round robin* technique is used as a variation of *round robin* in which each server has integer weight in proportion to the it's capacity. The servers are assigned requests in proportion to their weights [Ciardo,2001;Feldmann,1998].

In state aware policies, the dispatcher makes use of state information received from the client and/or server. Server state aware algorithms use server information e.g. server load to assign requests to the servers. The *shortest queue* algorithm and the *dynamic weighted round robin* techniques are the examples of state aware algorithms. In the *shortest queue* technique, the server with minimum load is selected for dispatching the current request. In the *dynamic weighted round robin* technique, dynamic weights are assigned to the servers in proportion to the server state. Weights are computed periodically and incremented when a new connection is assigned. Client state aware algorithms are more sophisticated as they examine the HTTP request. Information in the URL may be used for different purposes e.g. cache affinity to use locality of reference or to make use of services provided by some specialized servers [Gadde,2001]. In client and server state aware policies, the dispatcher assigns requests to the servers on the basis of combined state of the server and the client. Client state aware policies are easier to implement as compared to server state aware policies [Androlini,2002; Cardellini,2002].

Main requirements of a good load balancing service are [Othama,2003]:

(a) Replication transparency of servers: For improved performance, scalability and reliability, distributed applications are replicated on many servers. But existence of multiple servers must be concealed from users and programmers. Transparency is one of the major design goals of the DCS. Load balancing service should be designed to communicate with the applications and accept load control requests from it without modifications in server application software.

(b) Stateful servers for distributed applications: A stateful server maintains the current status of the requests between subsequent calls by the client to the server. In case of stateless servers, servers does not maintain any information about clients. Stateless servers have distinct advantages of scalability and fault tolerance. However, a load balancer must have state information of the replicas, particularly in heterogeneous environment, for marshalling operation which is required in case of difference in data representation formats [Sinha,2001].

(c) Fault tolerance using decentralized load balancing: Centralized load balancing algorithms are simple. But in case of failure, load balancing service will be disrupted.

Fault tolerance in load balancing may be achieved by using decentralized load balancing. This will also enhance scalability and reliability of the load balancing system.

(d) Diverse load monitoring algorithms: The load level on a distributed application may vary frequently within a given period of time. These variations may be unpredictable. In case of different load conditions, it is desirable to use different load balancing algorithms. For example, in case of heavy load level, fine grain services are suitable [Chen,2001].

(e) Dynamic replica activation: Depending on varying load levels, e.g. in case of increased load condition, additional replicas may be added to the system and vice versa. Load balancing service must be able to support dynamic creation and termination of such replicas. This will provide more flexible load balancing.

5.2 LOAD BALANCING OF CLUSTER SERVER

Primary objective of most of the existing research is to find ways of improving performance by minimizing request execution time, minimizing communication and other overheads and/or maximizing resource utilization in conjunction with fairness in job execution. I/O scheduling is also an important criteria in measuring performance. With the improvement in processing speed and main memory size, I/O subsystem impose a significant bottleneck that prevents applications from achieving maximum system utilization. Problems in implementing I/O based load balancing algorithms in a server cluster are that they require mechanism to collect and analyze the data thereby incurring in potentially expensive overheads and large amount of state information [Kartza,2003; Eindnerger,2000].

Scheduling algorithms have substantial impact on performance of the system. The complexity of workload characteristics requires robust load balancing policies. The client requests rates fluctuate dramatically even within short periods of times due to wide disparity in processor and I/O resource requirements of requests. Adapting a load balancing policy to schedule workload without human intervention is critical for swift operation of the cluster of servers. Workload on a server is determined by the amount of time needed to execute all the requests received from the clients in the system. But ideally, the workload cannot be accurately measured before the requests are actually processed. Therefore, it is necessary to use techniques to measure the load by using other parameters like the queue length and utilization of the processor.The following scheduling policies are considered for distributing client requests among servers:

5.2.1 Random

In random allocation policy, the incoming requests are forwarded to a randomly selected server. Each of the servers has equal probability of getting the request. The algorithm may result in poor performance. *Random* method can also be extended to solve the heterogeneity issue servers [Mitzenmacher,1997; Mitzenmacher,2001].

5.2.2 Round Robin

This algorithm rotates through a list of servers. Address of any one of the servers can be mapped to a client request. All the servers are treated equally regardless of the number of connections to the server or its response time. Advantages of round robin algorithm are that it is simple, cheap and predictable. Although this algorithm gives better results, it may not be sufficient for heterogeneous group of servers, as this method does not take into account the servers capability. The algorithm has no knowledge of current status of the server workload, software or applications. Also, it does not have information about availability of the servers. It is assumed that the incoming client requests do not have any affinity to a specific server. Figure 5.3 shows the order of execution or requests in round robin method.

5.2.3 Weighted Round Robin

This algorithm tries to eliminate the deficiencies of simple round robin method by pre-assigning static weights to each server. This is done by assigning each server numerical weights between 1 and 10. Capacity of a server can be considered as a static parameter. A server will be assigned load in proportion to its weight. To use weight-based algorithm, relative weights are assigned carefully to each server instance. Weights may be determined on the basis of server configuration, for example, processing capacity of the server's hardware in relation to other servers. If the weight of a server is changed and it is rebooted, new information is propagated throughout the cluster.

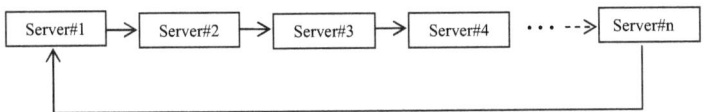

Fig. 5.3: Round robin scheduling for web servers

For example, if test results indicate that Server#1 can process 100 requests per second, Serve#2 as well as Server#3 can process 200 requests per second, Server#4 can process 300 requests per second and Server#5 can process 500 requests per second than the weights should be 1 2 2 3 5 for servers Server#1, Server#2, Server#3, Server#4 and Server#5 respectively. This means that out of 13 requests, Server#1 will get 1 request, Server#2 will each get 2 requests, Server#3 will get 2 requests, Server#4 will get 3 requests and Server#5 will get 5 requests. However, just like *round robin* technique, weighted round robin algorithm does not consider the processing time of clients' individual request. In the situations where some of the requests take longer time, advance load balancing algorithms are required. A variation of round robin technique is ***dynamic weighted round robin***, which dynamically evaluates weights based on the load state of the server. These weights are changed periodically. However, in all other policies, requests' allocation algorithms have no knowledge of the system's current state.

5.2.4 Shortest Queue

At each server's processor, a queue of incoming request is maintained. In a simple case, the server with minimum number of requests at its processor queue is assigned the new request. But if the requests have too much variation in their processing time, then simply measuring queue length is not sufficient. In such situations, we have to approximate the processing time requirement of each request and the load on the processor is the summation of processing time requirements of the requests in the queue. However, this technique has theoretical significance only as it is not possible to determine exact execution time requirement before actually running the process. We may only find estimate of execution time using statistical techniques like exponential smoothening or identify long processes which have already used execution time more than the average execution time of the processes. Estimates can also be developed by benchmarking of server performance based on real time statistics to determine load level of the server. However such estimates must be constantly updated over time [Goswami,1993].

5.2.5 Diffusive Load Balancing

The network of servers is stored in the form of graph G <V, E>. Here, V is the number of server nodes and E represents communication links between nodes as shown in Fig 5.4 (a). Figure 5.4 (b) shows the representation of this graph by means of adjacency matrix.

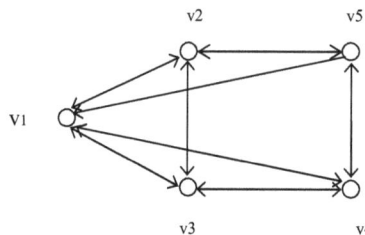

(a) Network topology for diffusive load balancing

$$G \begin{bmatrix} & V1 & V2 & V3 & V4 & V5 \\ V1 & 0 & 1 & 1 & 1 & 0 \\ V2 & 1 & 0 & 1 & 1 & 1 \\ V3 & 1 & 1 & 0 & 1 & 0 \\ V4 & 1 & 0 & 1 & 0 & 1 \\ V5 & 1 & 1 & 0 & 1 & 0 \end{bmatrix}$$

(b) Representation of the network by graph G <V, E>

Fig. 5.4: Graph representation on a network of servers

A request assigned at the server is forwarded to another server, if communication link exists between any two servers. The client request is received by the router, which, in turn, forwards request to one of the servers. The search for granting server causes traversal of the network along directed edges in diffusive fashion i.e. edges leading to less loaded servers. Request is moved from a server to its neighbouring server provided the difference of load between the server and its neighbour is above a threshold value. The workload of the server is measured using the length of processor's ready queue. The search finishes when the granting server is found. Performance indicators of load balancing are response time (time which is defined as the difference between finish time of execution of a request and the time when client submits that request), active connection count, server agent response, bandwidth consumption etc [Elsasser,2002; Sloklic,2002].

5.3 LOAD BALANCING METHODOLOGY

To illustrate the process of DLB of server cluster in the proposed framework, we describe the process formally as well as informally in following sub-sections.

5.3.1 Informal Description of the Algorithm

In this algorithm, it is assume that:

(a) The scheduler has perfect information while making scheduling decisions.

(b) The scheduling overheads are negligible.

(c) The requests are highly independent and they can be executed at any time and in any order.

(d) A closed queuing network model is considered.

There are n independent processors, each serving its queue and interconnected by high-speed network with negligible communication delay. We examine the system for $n=5$ processors which is reasonable for medium scale departmental network. The workload is shared among the replicated servers. The arrived requests are scheduled on the servers. In a server queue, requests are executed using round robin method.

Almost all the load balancing schemes use some load indices to measure the server load levels. Prior studies have shown that resource queue lengths are good indicator of load levels [Ferrari,1987]. We use sum of execution times of active server accesses as the server load index in shortest queue policy. Server on which a request will be executed is decided by a particular algorithm as follows:

(a) In random policy, a server will be selected randomly with each server having equal probability.

(b) In round robin policy, a list of servers is maintained and requests are assigned to the servers in the circular fashion.

(c) In weighted round robin policy, each server is assigned number of requests in proportion to the weight of the server.

(d) In shortest queue policy, a server having minimum number of requests in its queue, will be forwarded a request.

(e) In diffusive algorithm, a request assigned at a server is forwarded to another adjacent server if communication linked exists between the two servers and the new server has lesser load.

Compute the load on a server as:

$$W_i = \sum_{j=1}^{p_i} t_j \qquad (1)$$

Where,

t_j is the service time of the request j

p_i is the number of processes on node i

W_i is the workload on server i

The status of each server is computed upon arrival of a new request.

The response ratio R of a process is computed as:

$$R = t / (t + w) \qquad 0 < R <= 1 \qquad (2)$$

Where,

t is the service time of the request

w is the waiting time or missed time

We have used two load indices, queue length on the server and utilization of the processor.

Processor utilization is computed as:

$$U_{mean} = \left(\sum_{i=1}^{n} U_i\right) / n \qquad (3)$$

Where,

U_{mean} is the mean utilization.

U_i is the utilization of server i

n is the number of servers

Mean response time:

$$R_{mean} = \left(\sum_{i=1}^{n} R_i\right) / n \qquad (4)$$

Where,

R_{mean} is the mean response time

R_i is the response time of server i

Standard deviation of the response time is:

$$\sigma(R_i) = \text{sqrt}\left(\sum (R_i - R_{mean})^2\right) / n \qquad (5)$$

Load balancer collects load index information from each server so that the systems load distribution l is

$$l = \{ l_i \mid 0 <= i <= n \} \qquad (6)$$

Load distribution at time t is described by the mean value

$$l_{mean} = \left(\sum_{i=1}^{n} l_i \right) / n \qquad (7)$$

and the variance:

$$\sigma(L_i) = \left(\sum_{i=1}^{n} (l_i - l_{mean}) \right) / n \qquad (8)$$

This load information is collected from all servers periodically. Load balancing on each server is formalized by random arrival time and random service time. We can also measure the inaccuracy in load measurement. Load inaccuracy for certain delay Δt is defined as the statistical mean of difference in queue lengths measured at arbitrary time t and t+Δt. When the server is moderately busy, say 50%, the load inaccuracy is only moderate even with high delay. But when server is too busy, say 90%, the load index accuracy is much more. Therefore, at higher load levels, information dissemination delays should be small otherwise the results will have higher magnitude of errors [Xu,1993]. Communication overheads may also be computed as:

$$C_o = t_c / mst \qquad (9)$$

Where,

C_o is the communication overhead

t_c is the sum of time to send load from node *i* to the supervisor and time to receive message from the supervisor

mst is the mean service time

Value of t_c can be computed as:

$$t_c = t_s + t_r \qquad (10)$$

Where,

t_s is the sending time

t_r is the receiving time

Migration overhead may be computed as:

$$m_o = t_m / mst \qquad (11)$$

t_m is time to migrate a request from source to destination and includes time for queue manipulation, load table operations etc.

Equation (1) to Equation (11) constitute steps in the formal algorithm. A centralized load balancer performs load balancing request distribution by selecting appropriate server. The performance of load balancing algorithm is measured on the basis of response time achieved by using a given algorithm.

The following steps are involved in the algorithm:

(a) Accept the new client request: The request is submitted to admission control mechanism which determines whether there is sufficient capacity to service the request. If sufficient capacity is not available, the request is rejected. Otherwise the request is forwarded to the load balancer.

(b) **Collect the state information:** The load balancer collects the status of the servers to find the load information and performance weights etc. depending on the algorithm used for load balancing.

(c) **Server selection**: Select the server which is going to process the request.

(d) **Request distribution:** Forward the request to the selected server. In case of stateful servers, the load balancer transfers the state of the client from previous server to the selected server.

5.3.2 Formal Algorithm

The algorithm for server load balancing is formally described as under:

Algorithm *Server-Load-Balancing*

/*Algorithm for load balancing a server cluster. Following techniques have been used: 1=Random, 2=Round Robin, 3=Shortest Queue, 4=Diffusive*/

{

for each server in the cluster store following data

server-queue, number-of-processes, server-load, mean-response- ratio, server-utilization

for each request store

pid, ser-time, arr-time, dep-time, response-time

/* *new requests arrive at load balancer randomly with random service time requirements*/

CreateLoadBalancerQueue(struct *processes*())

RandomAlloction(queue *lbq*, queue *server*())

    {

    for each process in the load balancer queue

        assign a request p_i from *lbq* to server S_j;

        increment i and j;

        if the *serverlist* is finished assign $i=1$;

    }

RoundRobinAllotment(queue *lbq*, queue *server*());

    {

    for each process in the load balancer queue

        assign a request p_i from *lbq* to server S_j;

        increment i and j;

        if the *serverlist* is finished

            assign $i=1$;

    }

ShortestQueueAllocation(queue *lbq*, queue *server*())

 { int *i, sid*=0, *bt,j,n*;

  for each process in the load balancer queue

   select a server S_i with minimum load;

   assign request p_i to S_i

 }

DiffusiveAllocation(queue *lbq*, queue *server*())

 {

 ComputeThreshold( );

  /*compute propagation threshold of the system */

 for each server in the *serverlist*

  assign request p_i from *lbq* to S_j;

  do while granting server is not found

   if (*server-load$_i$* - *server-load$_{i+1}$* > *threshold*)

    server=s(i)

 }

 }

End of Algorithm

5.3.3 Example

Equation (1) to Equation (11) constitute steps in the formal algorithm evaluate DLB in web servers. The simulator was driven using artificial workload instead of real workload. Artificial workloads have a greater flexibility as compared to real workloads and are easier to reproduce. Random process arrival and random service time distribution was assume. DCS with n homogeneous servers interconnected by high-speed network with negligible communication delays was consider. The system was examined with $n=5$.

Table 5.1: Computation of mean response time of the servers using different load balancing techniques

	Mean Response Time			
Server id	Random	Round Robin	Shortest Queue	Diffusive
1	285.5	252.6	157.20	180.1
2	268.2	126.4	150.67	161.2
3	76.1	101.8	151.25	113.6
4	172.9	200.8	154.98	170.2
5	83.1	93.9	126.9	141.2

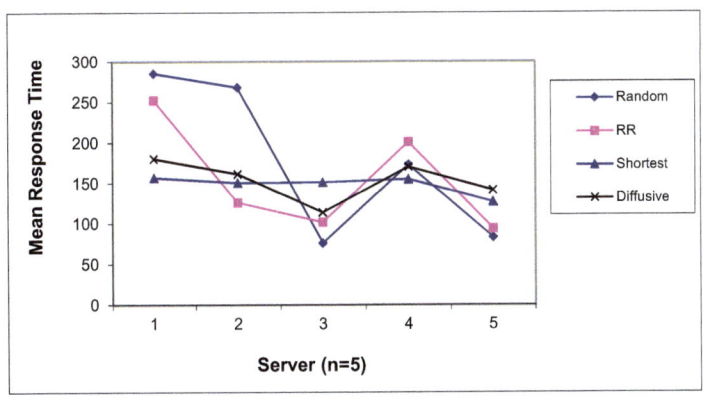

Fig. 5.5: Comparison of mean response time on each server using different load balancing techniques

Table 5.2: Computation of utilization of the servers using different load balancing techniques

	Utilization of Servers			
Server id	Random	Round Robin	Shortest Queue	Diffusive
1	46	83	77	79
2	89	81	80	73
3	98	61	79	81
4	79	82	76	69
5	81	38	70	76

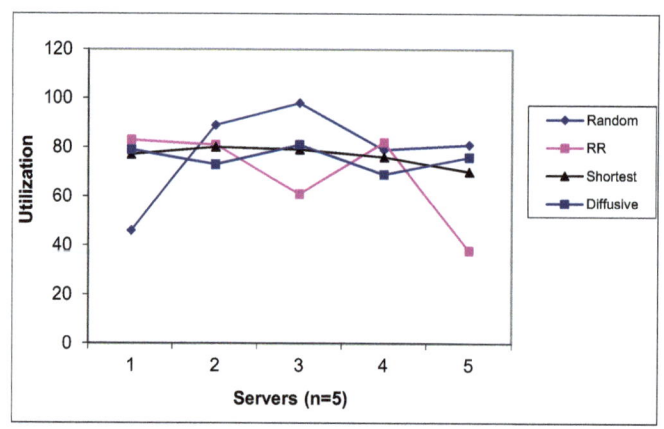

Fig. 5.6: Comparison of utilization of servers using different load balancing techniques

Table 5.3: Computation of mean response time of the servers for RR and WRR techniques

Mean Response Time			
Server id	Weight	Round Robin	Weighted Round Robin
1	2	278.1	163.3
2	1	279.2	152.6
3	1	277.8	155.9
4	1	291.8	144.7
5	2	266.8	147.1

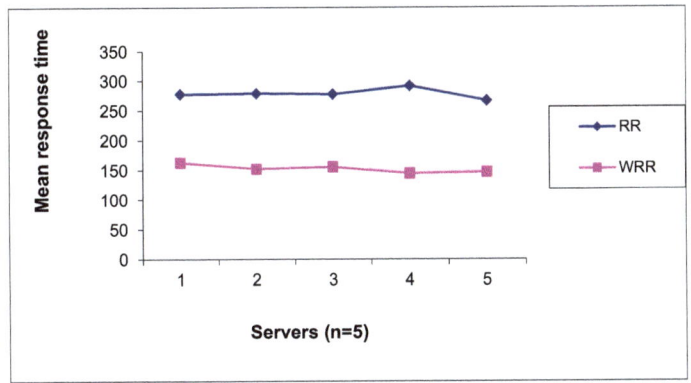

Fig 5.7: Comparison mean response time of the servers using RR and WRR techniques

Table 5.4: Computation of utilization of the servers for RR and WRR techniques

Utilization of Servers			
Server id	Weight	Round Robin	Weighted Round Robin
1	2	49	98
2	1	98	99
3	1	97	95
4	1	95	92
5	2	46	79

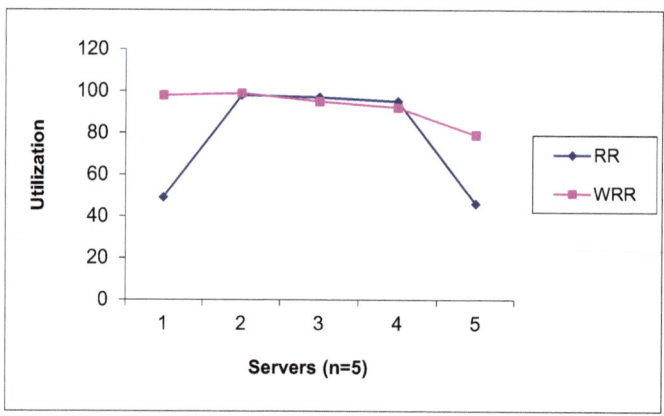

Fig. 5.8: Comparison utilization of the servers using RR and WRR techniques

The results of comparison of server load balancing techniques are shown in Table 5.1, Table 5.2, Fig. 5.5 and Fig. 5.5. Table 5.3, Table 5.4, Fig.5.7 and Fig .5.8 show the comparison of round robin and weighted round robin techniques. For each algorithm, mean response time and utilization of processor was computed. Load balancing techniques gives much better results than assigning requests to the servers randomly. Round robin method achieves moderate results compared to random load balancing. Weighted round robin technique yields better results than round robin in an environment with different server capabilities. As expected, the shortest queue algorithm gives best results but as it is not possible to know in advance the processing time for a client's request, this technique has only theoretical significance. However this technique works as a benchmark to compare other implementable techniques. The results also reveal that diffusive load balancing yield better result than round robin technique.

5.4 SUMMARY

Scheduling of jobs in web cluster of servers is a major research activity in DCS. One of the critical scheduling problems in distributed computing environment is load balancing on a cluster of replicated servers which faces a constant pressure of increased network traffic and diverse load levels. This problem is aggravated with the growing complexity of web based applications and services. A key issue in server load balancing in a DCS is to select an effective load balancing scheme to distribute clients' requests to the servers. Load balancing improves the performance of the server cluster by proper resource utilization and reducing the mean response time by distributing the workload evenly among the servers in the cluster. In this chapter, the problem of server load balancing are investigated and various server load balancing policies are evaluated. The policies considered are weighted round robin, shortest queue and diffusive load balancing. Performance of each of these policies was analyzed and compared. The objective is to identify the techniques that produce good overall system performance. On the basis of simulation results, it can be concluded that use of DLB algorithms is necessary to improve the performance of server cluster in network and web servers.

CHAPTER 6
EXPLORING DLB IN INFORMATION TECHNOLOGY

6.1 PREAMBLE

In this chapter, we have identified some challenges causing overload in the web based applications and necessitate the use of DLB in Information Technology. We have mainly raised the issues of public domain software, information overload, lack of optimization algorithms in routers, heterogeneity of end servers and incompatibility problem in servers. These issues make us aware of possible problems which may be encountered in future and provide a new direction to performance improvement techniques in distributed computing. We feel that such problems have been ignored by the computer science community and need urgent attention.

In recent years, web base applications have become huge and complex. They require dynamic computations and secure communication with large number of dispersed users. The distributed computational applications cannot be built with the help of traditional hardware. Large distributed computing applications have led to development of scalable clusters and grids that provide high performance computing resources. Clusters are becoming increasingly popular alternative to custom built parallel and monolithic architectures. Clusters' popularity is based on their ability to offer cost effective environment for running computation intensive parallel applications and are widely accepted as a viable alternative to tightly coupled parallel computers and mainframes. Clusters have been further empowered by open source software such as Linux and standards such as PVM (Parallel Virtual Machine) and MPI (Message Passing Interface). Clusters allow addition of nodes so that their computational power can be upgraded to meet the increasing demand of processing load. This expansion, however, leads to heterogeneity as and when the nodes and servers with better configuration are added. This increases the complexity of system administration. The use of self-organizing infrastructure is to react to exceptional situations proactively, as in case of overload of servers and nodes. DLB is one of the self-organizing techniques that can be effectively used to balance uneven workload on the cluster [Amiri,2000]. DLB technique distributes processing workload as evenly as possible among the nodes in a cluster. This helps in improving response time by minimizing job execution time, minimizing communication overheads and maximizing resource utilization. It also tries to preserve fairness in individual job execution. DLB allows cluster of nodes to be used as a cost effective alternative to mainframe computing. It is also used to balance the load in a cluster of web servers deployed by websites for processing clients' requests [Aron,2000; Fox,1997; Wolf,2001].

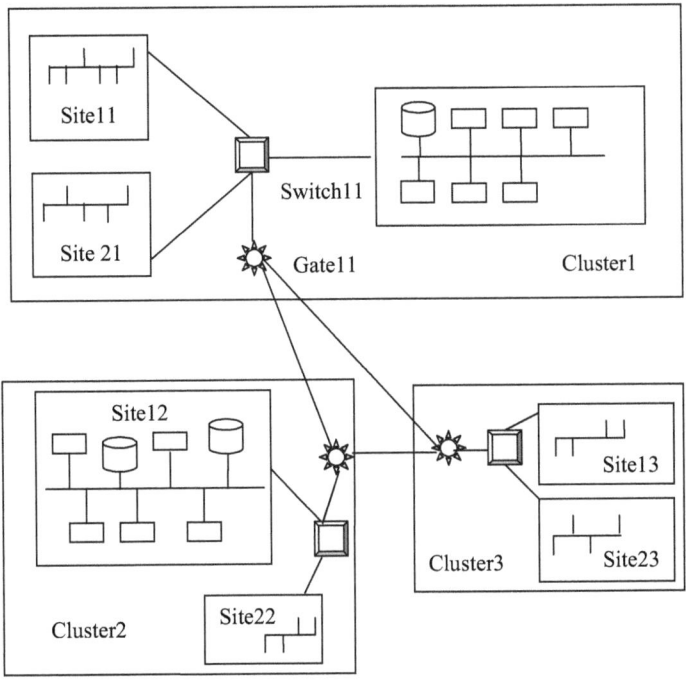

Fig. 6.1: A Computational Grid

A computational grid, as shown in Fig. 6.1, consists of a set of clusters that are interconnected by gates. Each cluster may contain several sites that are connected by switches. A site consists of a number of processing elements as well as storage devices interconnected over a local area network. Grid infrastructure enables integrated collaborative use of high performance systems, networks, databases and variety of end user devices that are owned and managed by multiple organizations [Baker,2002]. The objective is to provide computing utilities in the same manner as power utilities supply electric power. Similar objective was also dreamed way back in 1960s by means of MULTICS operating system project by the giants of that era viz. General Electric Company, MIT and Bell Labs. MULTICS was based on timesharing concept, but the dream could not be realized. Now, users draw their computing and storage power from grids rather than from local resources. Grid computing has been envisaged as the next revolution after WWW. A number of scientific and commercial applications have started harnessing grids [Foster,2001].

Major issues in grid computing software include workload management and efficient utilization of resources by improved distributed scheduling techniques which fall in the scope of load balancing. Heterogeneity due to involvement of variety of resources also demands implementation of load balancing in the grid environment [Yagobi,2006]. The integration of load balancing in grid middleware software is shown in Fig 6.2

6.2 RECENT CHALLENGES

In this section, we address new problems and challenges which are causing increased traffic and load imbalance in distributed applications.

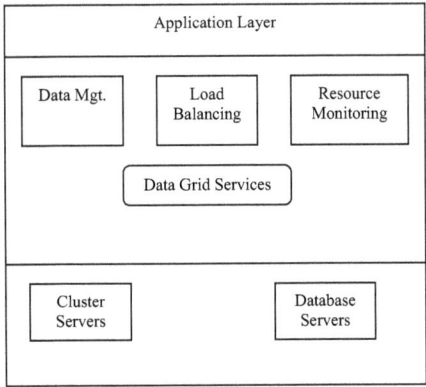

Fig. 6.2: Application of load balancing in grid architecture

6.2.1 Public Domain Software

Public domain software like Linux refer to the programs that are not copyrighted. Software are free and can be used without any restriction. The authors of the public domain software intended to share them. Public domain software have no owner as such. Even the governments do not own them. They are simply free. Anyone can modify and even sell the software. Freeware refer to fully working programs which anyone may use and redistribute for no cost whatsoever. Freeware may or may not be copyrighted. An author may ask that his software is not to be distributed or modified. Sharewares are try-before-you-use software. Sometimes a shareware contains a message asking for regular users to send merely a small fee to the author. Often it is a fully functional program with a time delay message asking for registration fee and the time delay message will be removed if registration code is entered [Detienne,2006; Gacek,2004].

Open source and free software products have challenged established licensing models for many types of mass market products e.g. OS, development tools, web servers and databases. GNU GPL (General Network Users General Public License) is intended to guarantee freedom to share and change free software. It allows free distribution and modifying but all derivatives must be under GNU GPL. Public domain software include OS, word processors, utility programs, indexers, languages, language subroutines and smart modem programs for data transfer using cable. These programs are very inexpensive as compared to commercial products [Williams,2002; Sack, 2003].

Linux is free Unix type of OS developed under the GNU GPL, whose source code is freely available to every one. Open source software together with small and low cost data centres provide cost effective alternative to centralized ISP setup consisting of sophisticated servers, expensive software, high capacity storage and bandwidth. Linux is a default choice for Internet server platforms as it is a robust, secure and high performance OS. It works on low cost servers, workstations and even old Pentiums. Web (Apache), proxy (Squid) and email (Sendmail) server applications are available free of cost on Linux [Williams,2002; Mundie,2002: Linux,2000]. Open source software, together with clusters and grids, have offered a cost effective environment for web-enabled applications. The extensive use of open source and public domain software is continuously increasing processing workload on the intranet and Internet. Load balancing can be effectively used to balance this workload on a cluster. Load balancing of certain services such as FTP and web servicing is must for any organization that needs to service a large client base. A load balancer can distribute connections among two or more servers, proportionately cutting the work each one has to do [Jessica,2003; Scacchi,2001].

6.2.2 Information Overload

The rapid growth of Internet and improved accessibility to web has presented users with huge amount of information. While tools for conducting business, communication and sharing information electronically have enabled companies to transact practically at the speed of light, they have also radically changed the way of conducting business. From communication programs for instant messaging and email to middleware and Linux, the technology is finally powerful and reliable to support freely networked business partnerships. The extended enterprises have ability to increase responsiveness by imposing performance constraints. The technology is causing information overload and it is becoming difficult to focus on some specific information. People have to face large volume of information which they are unable to attend. Machine generated data from variety of sources is increasing at an exponential rate and could hit 2000GB per person per year by the year 2020.

Getting access to data, determining its accuracy and quality and then knowing how to make good decision with the data across an extended enterprise is becoming difficult [Jinwan,2001]. Figure 6.3 depicts a large number of information sources eventually leading to information overload.

Initial benefits from search engine technology have been critically degraded over time by rapid increase in the number of Internet pages. Traditional retrieval strategies, therefore, yield poor results. Search engine users are increasingly experiencing information overload. Information overload has affected business productivity of an organization as well as work performance of individuals. Technical approaches to dealing with this problem have caused initial euphoria, yet have proved ineffective in solving the problem.

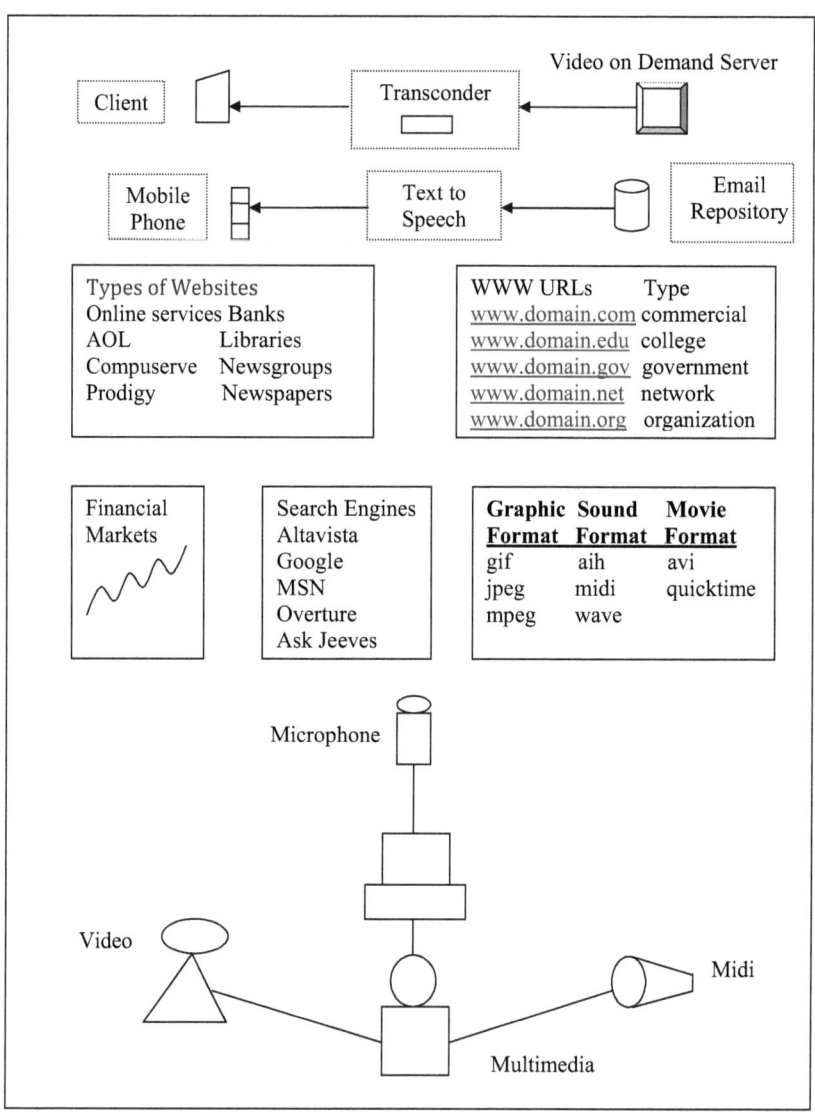

Fig. 6.3: Variety of information sources

Enhancement of user empowerment in the area of Internet based information retrieval must therefore focus on augmenting user capabilities. Issues of information literacy and information anxiety are explored relevant to non-professional users [Chados,2006].

6.2.3 Mismatch / Incompatibility of Severs

Breakthrough in software productivity depends on our ability to combine pieces of hardware and software to produce new applications. To make large and quality software rapidly, we need assembling of reusable building blocks into a new system rather than build-from-scratch techniques. Problems in composition are due to low-level issues of interoperability e.g. mismatches in programming languages, database schemas, operating platforms and other components on servers. Server mismatch exposes some fundamental problems and suggests possible research avenues to solve them. There may be conflicting assumptions about protocols, data models for RPC, topology, the type of user interfaces etc [Garlan,1995].

In addition to above components, many intermediaries are also supported for WWW. Intermediaries are the software entities deployed on Internet for flow of information from clients to the servers, among clients and among servers to cope with end user information overloading, support for mobile access, content personalization and infrastructural support for ubiquitous services like personal digital assistants (PDAs), thin clients, mobile phones etc. They are used for caching, filtering, indexing and transconding. The server mismatch problem is expected to grow further with the increasing application of these intermediaries.

High performance is one of the critical requirements demanded by mission critical applications such as finance, manufacturing etc. which are running on server clusters. Mismatch between OS and distinct characteristics of server applications is key performance bottleneck. Although servers have become very powerful with huge memory and disk space, it may be difficult to achieve satisfactory level of performance even after extensive system tuning efforts.

In the process management for large server clusters, the major issue is scheduling of thousands of processes. For effectively scheduling such a large number of processes, intelligent scheduling decisions are desirable, e.g. preemptive processor scheduling may degrade the performance of some applications. One example is of database applications, which uses an efficient mutual exclusion technique called latches to synchronize access to shared data. If a process holding a latch is preempted by round robin scheduler, the process will join at the end of the ready queue. It is probable that the next process scheduled to run may also require latches, and therefore not able to use its time quantum. For taking intelligent decision, the scheduler must have application dependent information. Scheduler needs to have semantic information about applications and their execution states. User level threads can be also be used to avoid unnecessary context switches inside the kernel. User level threads are provided by a thread package, which allows users to implement their own algorithm to the schedule the threads within the allocated time quantum. Even if a thread executes a system call, other thread in the process can continue to execute [Kanungo,2005]. Load balancing can be very useful in for scheduling processes across the servers in a cluster. Appropriate admission control and request distribution mechanism can be used for processing requests efficiently. Content aware scheduling algorithms for distributing client requests can be helpful in taking intelligent scheduling decisions depending on the type and capabilities of the servers [Kanungo,2006d].

6.2.4 Lack of Optimization Algorithm in Routers

Routers are used in heterogeneous networks to interconnect two different technologies and forward data packets between them. Routing is the act of moving information across the internetwork from a source node to the destination node. Along the way, at least one node is typically encountered. Routers determine the optimal routing path in the network and transport the packets through an internetwork called packet switching network. Routing protocols use metrics to evaluate what path will be best for a packet to travel. Different routers may use different matrices like path length, load on network resources, bandwidth, routing delay, reliability of network, communication cost etc. To aid to the process of path determination, routing algorithm uses a routing table which contains some routing information about the next hop or destination address. It may also contain other information like desirability of a path. When router receives an incoming packet, it checks the destination address and attempts to associate this address with the next hop. Operations in a router are depicted by means of Fig. 6.4.

Routers communicate with one another and update their routing tables through transmission of variety of messages. The router update message is one such messages that consists of all or portion of routing table. By analyzing routing update messages from all other routers, a router can build a detailed picture of network topology. Another message, called link state advertisement, Router informs other routers about the state of the sender's links.

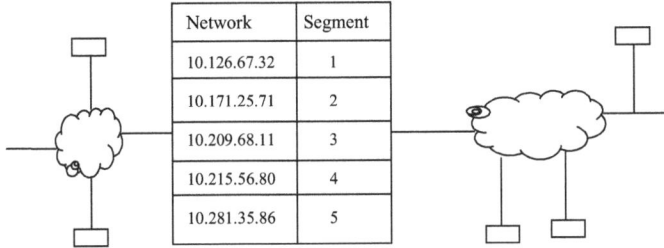

Fig. 6.4: Operation of the router in a network

This message can also be used to build complete picture of the network topology to determine the optimal route of a network destination. Switching algorithms are also used in routers and are generally same for most routing protocols. In most of the cases, a host determines router address and sends packet to this address along with the protocol address of the destination host. The next hop may not be ultimate destination host but again a router which executes the same switching process. As the packet moves through the network, its physical address changes but its protocol address remains the same [Anderson,2000].

Various routing algorithms exist and each algorithm has a different impact on network and router resources. Optimality is the most desirable feature of routing algorithms. It is the capability of a routing algorithm to select best route to transfer a packet. The algorithm uses matrix weighing to make calculations. Some algorithms use number of hops and delays. Weight given to different matrices may also vary. One algorithm may give more weight to the number of hops while another algorithm gives weight to delay. The algorithm should also be able to converge rapidly. Convergence is the process of agreement by all other routers on optimal path. Most of the router algorithms use dynamic routing i.e. they adjust to changing network circumstances by analyzing incoming routing update messages. If a message indicates that network change has occurred, the algorithm recalculates the route and sends new routing update message. These messages permeate through the network, stimulating routers to re-execute their algorithms and change their routing tables accordingly. Some of the sophisticated routing protocols support multiple paths to the same destination to allow traffic multiplexing over multiple lines to improve reliability and throughput [Aversa,2000; Hunt,1998].

Internet bandwidth explosion and advent of complex distributed applications had presented new challenges for routers. These challenges include more throughput, more computations and more flexibility. In minimal routing algorithms, which try to choose shortest path for each packet, load imbalance may be caused due to heavy load on some links and less load on other [Newman,1997].

Load balancing can be implemented at OS level, at middleware level or at the network level. Routers help to achieve load balancing at network level. To improve worst case traffic, routing algorithms must balance load by sending some of the load over non-optimal paths also. Load balancing can be incorporated in routers to distribute traffic over all the router ports that are at the same distance from destination address. Load balancing increases utilization of network segments and consequently effective network bandwidth. Load balancing algorithms can be implemented in many ways in routers and at various levels of networking protocol stack [Phillips,1991; Shi,2005].

6.2.5 Performance and Heterogeneity of End Servers

In a client server environment, it is common to have a cluster of replicated servers which accepts processing requests from the large number of clients. As seen in Section 6.1, a cluster is a group of servers with identical contents, networked together to act as a single virtual server and capable of growing with corporate needs [Watts,1998].

For some organizations, a few servers and storage devices are sufficient which are easily manageable. But the organizations that support wider spectrum of applications and requirements, have developed a framework where capability of server is matched to the type of application. This is called n-tier architecture. The first tier contains external interface for request processing, supporting Internet applications such as web servers, firewalls, caching mechanism etc. The server architecture can be relatively simple. These applications do not require much integration with rest of the infrastructure. The second tier of servers contains application specific servers supporting mission critical applications. The servers require greater functionality to support varying demands from applications. Often scale up server configuration may be required. Number of processors is usually more and system performance between input/output and computations has to be balanced. Applications may be highly interdependent and may require better tuning compared to first tier applications. The third and final tier is database layer where large servers are needed for sophisticated database products. These servers are multiprocessor-based with rich functionality due to extensive processing needs e.g. online transaction processing (OLTP), data warehousing etc. Figure 6.5 shows a three-tier structure of a server cluster [Kephart,2003].

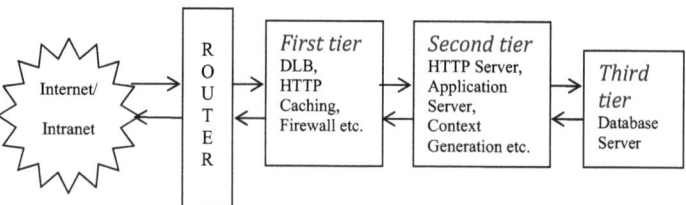

Fig. 6.5: Three-tier architecture of a server cluster

Heterogeneity within group of servers used in three-tier architecture of a server cluster raises the problem of how to distribute clients' requests to the different cluster nodes. The workload consisting of incoming requests is to be distributed evenly among the servers in the cluster [Aron,2000; Binachini,2000]. For a heterogeneous server cluster to achieve its high performance and high availability potential, DLB techniques are required. Combining load balancing with cluster of low cost servers is most cost effective, flexible and reliable strategy for web based services. Cluster load management software should efficiently support heterogeneous hardware environment and changing system configurations. Distribution of requests among servers can be implemented by monitoring the servers regularly and directing these requests dynamically to the least loaded servers. The capability of servers has to be taken into account while distributing the requests [Shaikh,1999]. DLB feature can be added to the pre-existing domain name service as it plays a crucial role in resolving client requests. DLB optimizes request distribution among servers based on factors like server capacity, current load and historical performance. It also improves mean response time and overall throughput of a DCS [Lu,1996].

6.2.6 Threats and Viruses

Internet has transformed the ways of doing business. Organizations in present e-business environment have to open up their private network applications and information assets to their customers, business partners and employees. This vast network and its associated technologies have introduces number of security threats from which organizations and users must protect themselves. Important data may be lost, privacy can be violated and the computer may be even used by an outside attacker to attack other computers on the Internet. Security mechanisms are necessary for reliable communication. The Internet servers are protected by firewalls. All accesses are blocked by default and only legitimate traffic is allowed to pass through. Automated monitoring of firewall rules and routing entries is done. Backup and restore utilities are provided for crucial data.

Viruses are the most widely known security threats. Viruses are malicious programs designed to replicate themselves, unnoticed of users, and infect their computers. Viruses keep running in the background as long as the computer is switched on. To protect from viruses, security features can be incorporated at OS level or antivirus software may be used. The term hacker means individual, who, electronically gains illegal access to data and try to manipulate it. Hackers may have variety of goals e.g. financial gain, spreading viruses etc. Spam is unsolicited mail often promoting products of a dubious financial or sexual nature and is a major cyber threat which may cause jamming of individual mailboxes, denial of service, attack on servers and can spread viruses. Torjan is a program, which does not replicates or copies itself but perform some illicit activity when it is executed. It stays inside the computer memory to damage it or enables a remote site to take control of the computer.

Virus writers and hackers are creating and distributing *viruses* and *trojans* for their own reasons while end users machines and networks are under constant threat of hacker attacks. The need of authentication and security has increased the complexity of middleware and application software. A web server that provides dynamic or secure content may incur significant performance penalty. E-commerce applications, which execute personal and commercial transactions, require data encryption. Supporting encrypted transactions on the web can be many times more expensive than insecure contents. The need of authentication and security places additional computational load on web servers making the use of load balancing necessary.

6.3 SOLUTIONS

DLB is an important research theme owing to the development of ever growing distributed computing applications. The areas described above pose challenges for further research and provide us opportunities to come up with new ideas.

We have described algorithm for DLB for a cluster of nodes to effectively utilize the processing power of nodes and improve the response ratio of processes in the system. This algorithm considers threshold level of the nodes to identify heavily loaded nodes and lightly loaded nodes. The processes are transferred from heavily loaded node to lightly loaded nodes dynamically. We have also studied various parameters for effective load measurement. These parameters called load indices are used to collect load information of nodes in a cluster continuously to identify overloaded nodes, underloaded nodes and processes to be transferred

We have presented an algorithmic infrastructure for efficient process migration. We have also compared suitability of non-preemptive and preemptive process migration for DLB and found that preemptive migration algorithm results in effective resources utilization provided we are able to identify long processes on overloaded nodes and transfer them to the underloaded nodes.

Problem of server load balancing has been investigated. Performance of various algorithms is also been compared. We found that shortest queue algorithm gives best result but the algorithm has only theoretical significance, however, it can act as a benchmark. Among the implementable algorithms, diffusive algorithm gives better results.

The methodologies and algorithms for DLB proposed in Chapter 2 and for process migration proposed in Chapter 4 can easily be incorporated in public domain operating systems for improving the performance in cluster of nodes. Routing algorithms can also be modified to incorporate features of DLB. Load balancing methodology for server cluster proposed in Chapter 5 can be useful to solve the performance and heterogeneity problems in servers. Algorithms need variations so that they can be used for solving information overload and server incompatibility problems. These variants have to be implemented while keeping the methodologies of DLB.

Load balancing is known to be a NP hard problem. Therefore, heuristic based search strategies for load balancing and cluster partitioning can be developed to meet the new challenges in Information Technology applications. There is a possibility of using intelligent optimization techniques in load balancing using heuristic search methods.

6.4 FUTURE SCOPE

DLB is challenging area of research in distributed computing. These areas include:

(1) Complexity in load balancing algorithms: Load balancing problem is known to be NP hard. Therefore, heuristic based search strategies for load balancing and cluster partitioning can be developed. We will investigate the possibilities of using intelligent optimization techniques in load balancing using heuristic search methods [Devine,2005; Chen,2002].

(2) DLB library for parallel applications: To provide a set of load balancing methods for application developers and researchers, a library can be useful. This library should also be able to support process and data migration. This library may enable DLB to produce partitions with size compatible with the capabilities of computational resources for a computing cluster [Devine,2005].

(3) Content aware load balancing: DLB algorithms should be able to extract information from web requests and use the contents for load balancing purpose. For example, the information in URL may be used for different purposes like cache affinity to use locality of reference or to exploit the services provided by some specialized servers depending upon the requirement of requests [Cardellini,2002; Yang,2000].

(4) Load balancing strategies for heterogeneous cluster and grids: Clusters and grids are becoming increasingly popular alternative to custom built parallel computers. Cluster

popularity is based on their ability to offer cost effective environment for running computation intensive parallel applications. Clusters allow addition of nodes so that their computational power can be enhanced to meet the increasing demand of processing load. Clusters have been further empowered by open source software such as Linux and standards such as PVM and MPI. The ability of expansion in a cluster, however, leads to heterogeneity due to addition of nodes with better configuration. Load balancing can be effectively used to balance uneven workload on a cluster. Tasks submitted to clusters and grids can be very diversified and irregular. The properties of clusters and grids make the load balancing problem more complex as compared to load balancing in parallel and distributed systems and need to be resolved [Foster, 2001; Yagobi,2006].

(5) Diffusion schemes for load balancing: One of the heuristic-based strategies for load balancing is diffusive load balancing in which load is moved from an overloaded node to neighboring under loaded node. The process is repeated iteratively until considerable balance is achieved. The concept, however, needs further investigations [Elsasser,2002].

(6) Topology driven load balancing schemes: We can develop a mechanism to describe the interconnection topology of the networks and their capabilities so that effective load balancing schemes may be developed for specific topologies [Yagobi,2006].

(7) Neural network based load balancing algorithm: Load balancing algorithms may be based on self learning of performance of each node and requests may be distributed among the server in the cluster based on their execution statistics.

(8) New challenges in DLB of IT applications: The solutions proposed in the thesis are useful for solving the problems mentioned in Chapter 6 like public domain software, heterogeneity of servers and router load balancing. However, using DLB technique to solve information overload, servers incompatibility and security problems need further variations while keeping methodologies of DLB[Kanungo,2006e].

(9) Desirable characteristics of load balancing algorithms: Load balancing services have to address many issues like replication transparency, stateless servers, load monitoring granularity, fault tolerance, decentralization of load balancing and extensibility of load balancing algorithms which are yet to be resolved. These features should be incorporated in order to increase the performance, scalability and reliability of the distributed applications that are becoming increasingly complex, broader and dynamic in their behaviour [Othama,2003].

(10) Input/output aware load balancing: Due to huge speed mismatch between central processing units and disks in modern systems, disk access is a major performance bottleneck resulting in poor speed of I/O intensive applications like databases, long simulations etc. DLB for I/O intensive cluster and storage area networks may make it possible to improve utilization in disks apart from improvement in utilization of processors and main memory [Qin,2004].

(11) Load balancing algorithms for routers: Load balancing can be implemented at the network level with the help of routers. Load balancing can be incorporated in routing algorithms to distribute traffic over all the router ports that are at the same distance from destination address. This increases utilization of network segments and consequently effective network bandwidth [Desell,2004; Shi,2005].

6.5 CONCLUDING REMARKS

This book has a wide scope in the field of distributed computing systems. The scope includes cluster of nodes and workstations, server cluster, computational grid, multiprocessors and even routers. In addition to the theoretical interest, algorithmic infrastructures and methodologies the book has applications in practical fields in distributed operating systems which are yet under research and development stage. They can also be incorporated in existing popular operating systems like Windows and Linux. These algorithms can be useful in increasing the resource utilization and response times of existing sites without adding extra hardware cost as we mainly emphasize on utilizing the existing infrastructure rather than upgrading the hardware facilities.

REFERENCES

[Abdelzaher,2000]

Abdelzaher, T. F. and Lu, C., "Modeling and Performance Control of Internet Servers," *39th IEEE Conference on Decision and Control,* Sydney, Australia, Dec. 2000, pp. 2234-2239.

[Abdelzaher,2002]

Abdelzaher, T.F., Shin, K.G. and Bhatti, N., "Performance Guarantee for Web Server End Systems: A Control Theoretical Approach," *IEEE Transactions on Parallel and Distributed Systems*, Vol. 13, No. 1, Jan. 2000, pp. 80-96.

[Ahuja,2005]

Ahuja, S.P., Eaggen, R. and Jha, A.K., "A Performance Evaluation of Distributed Algorithms on Shared Memory and Message Passing Middleware Platforms," *Informatica*, Vol. 29, 2005, pp. 327-333.

[Alonso,1988]

Alonso, R. and Cova, L.L., "Sharing Jobs Among Independently Owned Processors," *Proceeding of 8th International Conference on Distributed Computing System, IEEE,* New York, June 1988, pp. 282-288.

[Amiri,2000]

Amiri, K. et al., "Dynamic Function Placement for Data Intensive Cluster Computing," *Proceedings of the 2000 USENIX Annual Technical Conference,* San Diego, CA, June 2000, pp. 1-16.

[Anderson,2002]

Anderson, D., Chase, J. and Vahadat, A., "Interposed Request Routing for Scalable Network Storage," *ACM Transactions on Computer Systems*, Vol. 20, No. 1, Feb. 2002, pp. 1-24.

[Andreolini,2002]

Andreolini, M. Colajanni, M. and Morselli, R., "Performance Study of Dispatching Algorithms in Multi-tier Web Architectures," *Performance Evaluation Review*, Vol. 30, No. 22, Sept. 2002, pp.10-20.

[Aravinthan,1999]

Aravinthan, V. et al., "Dynamic Load Balancing for Multi Physical Modeling Using Unstructured Meshes," *11th international Conference on Domain Decomposition Methods,* 1999, pp. 380-387.

[Aron,2000]

Aron, M. Druschel, P. and Zwaenepoel, W., "Cluster Reserves: A Mechanism for Resource Management in Cluster-Based Network Servers," *Proceedings of the ACM SIGMETRICS, 2000 International Conference on Measurement and Modeling of computer Systems,* Santa Clara, CA, Vol. 28, June 2000, pp. 99-101.

[Aversa,2000]

Aversa, L. and Bestavros, A., "Load Balancing a Cluster of Servers using Distributed Packet Rewriting," *Proceeding of the IEEE International Performance, Computing and Communications Conference,* Pheonix U.S.A., Feb. 2000, pp. 24-29.

[Aweya,2002]

Aweya, J. et al., "An Adaptive Load Balancing Scheme for Web Servers," *International Journal of Network Management,* Vol. 12, No.1, Jan-Feb 2002, pp. 3-39.

[Baker,2002]

Baker, M., Bhuyya, R. and Laforenza, D., "Grids and Grid Technologies for Wide-Area Distributed Computing," *International Journal of Software: Practice and Experience (SPE),* Vol. 32, No. 15, 2002, pp. 1437-1466.

[Bakshi,1997]

Bakshi, Y. et al., "Overload Control in a Distributed System," *Proceedings of 15th International TeleTraffic Congress,* Washington, D.C., 1997, pp. 571-582.

[Ballintijn,2002]

Ballintijn, G., Van Steen, M. and Tanenbauum, A.S., "Characterizing Internet performance to Support Wide-area Application Development," *Operating System Review,* Vol. 34, No.4, Oct. 2002, pp. 42-47.

[Barak,1993]

Barak. A., Shai, G. and Wheeler, R.G., The Mosix Distributed Operating Systems: Load Balancing for UNIX, *Springer Verlag,* 1993.

[Barford,2001]

Barford, P. and Crovella, M.E., "Critical Path Analysis of TCP Transactions," *IEEE/ACM Transactions on Networking*, Vol. 9, No., June 2002, pp. 238-248.

[Berman,1996]

Berman, F. et al., "Application Level Scheduling on Distributed Heterogeneous Networks," ACM/IEEE Conference on *Supercomputing*, Pittsburg, PA, Nov. 1996, pp. 39-58.

[Binachini,2000]

Binachini, R. and Carrera, E.V., "Analytical and Experimental Evaluation of Cluster-Based WWW Severs," *World Wide Web Journal*, Vol. 3, No.4, Dec. 2000.

[Blumofe,1994]

Blumofe, R.D. and Park, D.S., "Scheduling Large Scale parallel Computations on Network of Workstations," *3rd IEEE International Symposium on High-Performance Distributed Computing*, San Francisco, CA, Aug. 1994, pp. 96-105.

[Bryhni,2000]

Bryhni, H. Klovning, E. and Kure, O.A., "A Comparison of Load Balancing Techniques for Scalable Web Servers," *IEEE Network*, Vol. 14, No. 4, Jul./Aug. 2000, pp. 58-64.

[Cardellini,2002]

Cardellini V. et al., "The State of Art Locally Distributed Web-Server Systems," *ACM Computing surveys*, Vol. 34, No.2, 2002, pp. 264-311.

[Cardellini,2000]

Cardellini, V., Colajanni, A. and Yu, P., "Geographic Load Balancing for Scalable Distributed Web Systems," *Proceedings of the International Symposium on Modeling, Analysis and Simulation of Computer and Telecommunication Systems. IEEE International performance,* San Francisco, CA, U.S.A., 2000, pp. 20-27.

[Carrera,2001]

Carrera, E.V. and. Bianchini, R., "Efficiency vs. Portability in Cluster based Network Servers," *Proceedings of 8th ACM SIGPLAN Symposium on Principles and Practices of Parallel Programming*, Snowbird, UT, June 2001, pp. 113-122.

[Casanova,1997]

Casanova, H., Dongarra J.J. and Moore K., Network Enabled Solvers and the NetSolve Project, 1997.

[Casavant,1994]

Casavant, T.L. and Kuhl, J.G., "A Taxonomy of Scheduling in General Purpose Distributed Systems," *IEEE Transactions on Software Engineering*, Vol.14, No.2, 1994, pp. 141-153.

[Castro,1999]

Castro, M. Dwyer M., Rumsewicz, M., "Load Balancing and Control for Distributed World Wide Web Servers," *Proceedings of IEEE International Conference on Control Applications*, Hawaii, USA, 22-27 Aug. 1999, pp.1614-1618.

[Chados,2006]

Chados, D. and Cohen, R., "A Method of Combining Email and Web Pages for Announcing Research Opportunities to Researchers," *ACM SIGMI–CPR '06*, Clarmont, California, USA, April 13-15, 2006, pp. 304-310.

[Chen,1995]

Chen, K., Bunt R.B. and Eager, D.L. "Write Caching in Distributed File Systems," *Proceedings of the 15th IEEE International Conference on Distributed Computing Systems*, Van Couver, BC, Canada, 1995, pp. 457-466.

[Chen,2002]

Chen, J. and Taylor, V.E., "Mesh Partitioning for Efficient Use of Distributed Systems," *IEEE Transactions Parallel and Distributed Systems*, Vol. 13, No. 1, 2002, pp. 67-79.

[Chen,2001]

Chen, X., Chen, H. and Mohapatra, P., "An Admission Control Scheme for Predictable Server Response Time for Web Accesses," *Proceedings of the 10th World Wide Web Conference*, Hong Kong, May 2001, pp. 545-554.

[Cherkasova,1998]

Cherkasova, and Phaal, P., "Session Based Admission Control: A Mechanism for Improving the Performance of an Overloaded Web Server," *Technical Report HPL-98-119, HP Labs*, June 1998.

[Ciardo, 2001]

Ciardo, G., Riksha, A. and Smimi, E., "EQUILOAD: A Load Balancing Policy for Cluster Web Servers," *Performance Evaluation*, Vol. 46, No. 2-3, 2001, pp. 101-124.

[Colajanni,1998]

Colajanni,M., Yu, P.S. and Dias, D.M., "Analysis of Task Assignment Policies in Scalable Distributed Web Server Systems," *IEEE Transactions on Parallel and Distributed systems*, Vol. 9, No. 6, 1998, pp. 585-600.

[Coulouris,1994]

Coulouris, G., Dollimore J. and Kingberg, T., Distributed Systems Concepts and Design, Addison Wesley, 1994.

[Cybenko,1989]

Cybenko, G., "Dynamic Load Balancing for Distributed Memory Multiprocessors," *Journal of Parallel and distributed Computing*, Vol. 7, No. 2, Oct. 1989, pp. 279-301.

[Dahlin,2000]

Dahlin, M., "Interpreting Stale Load Information," *IEEE Transaction on Parallel and distributed Systems*, Vol. 11, No. 10, Oct. 2000, pp. 1033-1047.

[De Couny,1994]

De Couny, H.L. et al., "Load Balancing for the Parallel Adaptive Solution of Partial differential Equations," *Applied Numerical Mathematics*, Vol. 16, No. 1-2, 1994, pp. 157-182.

[Degenaro,2000]

Degenaro, L. et al., "Middleware System Which Intelligently Caches Query Results," *Proceedings of ACM/IFIP Middleware*, Palisades, New York, April 2000, pp. 24-44.

[Desell,2004]

Desell, T., Maghraoui, K.E. and Varel, A, C., "Load Balancing of Autonomous Actors over Dynamic Networks," *Proceedings Hawaii International Conference on System Sciences*, Track 9, Vol. 9, Page 90268.1, 2004.

[Detienne,2006]

Detienne, F., Burkhardt, J.M. and Barcellini, F. "Open Source Software Communities: Current Issues," *CSI Communications*, Vol. 30, No. 5, 2006, pp. 12-16.

[Devarakonda,1989]

Devarakonda, M. and Iyer, R.K., "Predictability of Process Resource Usage: A Measurement based Study of Unix," *IEEE Transactions on Software Engineering*, Vol. 15, No. 12, Dec. 1989, pp. 1519-1586.

[Devine,2005]

Devine, K.D. et al., "New Challenges in Dynamic Load Balancing," *Applied. Numerical Mathematics,* Vol. 52, No. 2-3, 2005, pp. 133-152.

[Devine,1999]

Devine, K.D. et al., "Zoltan: A Dynamic Load Balancing Library for Parallel Applications," *User's Guide,* Sandia National Laboratories, Albuquerque, NM, 1999, Tech Report http: //www.cs.sandia.gov/Zoltan.

[Dittmann,2002]

Dittmann, G. and Herkersdorf, A. A., "Network Processor Load Balancing for High-Speed Links," *Proceedings of International Symposium on Performance Evaluation of Computer and Telecommunication Systems (SPECTS'2002),* San Diego, CA, Jul. 2002, pp. 727-735.

[Eager,1986]

Eager, D.L., Lazowska, E.D. and Zahorjan, J., "A Comparison of Receiver Initiated and Sender Initiated Adaptive Load Sharing," *Performance Evaluation,* Vol. 6, No. 5, 1988, pp. 662-675.

[Eager,1988]

Eager, D.L, Lazowska, E.D. and Zahorjan, J., "The Limited Performance Benefits of Migrating Active Processes for Load Sharing," *ACM SIGMETRICS Conference on Measuring and Modeling Computer Systems*, New York, 1988, pp. 662-675.

[Eindberger,2000]

Eindberger, W. et al., "Load Balancing Across Near Homogeneous Multi Resource Servers," *9th Heterogeneous Computing Workshop (HCW-2000),* Concun, Maxico, 2000, pp 60-71.

[Elsasser,2002]

Elsasser, R., Monien, C.B. and Preis, R., "Diffusive Schemes for Load Balancing on Heterogeneous Networks," *Theory of Computing System*, Vol. 35, 2002, pp. 305-320.

[Feldmann,1998]

Feldmann, A., Rexford, J. and Caceres, R., "Efficient Policies for Carrying Web Traffic Over Flow Switched Networks," *IEEE/ACM Transactions on Networks*, Vol. 6, No. 6, Dec. 1998, pp. 673-685.

[Feik,2005]

Feik, J. et al., "A Model for Resource Aware Load Balancing on Heterogeneous Clusters," *Technical Report CS-05-01*, Williams College, Department of Computer Science, 2005.

[Feller,2002]

Feller, J. and Fitzgerald, B., Understanding Open Source Software Development, Addison Wesley, 2002.

[Ferrari,1986]

Ferrari, D. and Zhou, S., "A Load Index for Dynamic Load Balancing," Proceedings of *ACM/IEEE Fall Joint Computer Conference*, Dallas, Texas, U.S.A., 1986, pp. 684-690.

[Ferrari,1987]

Ferrari, D. and Zhou, S., "An Empirical Investigation of Load Indices for Load Balancing Applications," *Proceedings of Performance*, North Holland, Netherlands, 1987, pp. 515-528.

[Finkel,1988]

Finkel, R. A., "An Operating Systems Vade Mecum," *Prentice Hall*, New Jersey, 1988.

[Foster,2001]

Foster, I., Kesselman, C. and Tuecke, S., "Anatomy of the Grid: Enabling Scalable Virtual Organizations," *International Journal of High Performance Computing Applications*, Vol. 15, No. 3, 2001, pp. 200-222.

[Fox,1997]

Fox, A. et al., "Cluster Based Scalable Network Services," *Proceedings of the 16th ACM Symposium on Operating Systems Principles*, St. Malo, France, Oct. 1997, pp. 78-91.

[Fu,2003]

Fu, B. and Tari, Z. A, "Dynamic Load Distribution Strategy for Systems Under High Task Variation and Heavy Traffic," *Proceedings of the ACM Symposium on Applied Computing,* Melbourne, Florida, pp. 1031-1037.

[Gacek,2004]

Gacek, C. and Arief, B., "The Many Meanings of Open Source," *IEEE Software*, Vol. 21, No. 1, 2004, pp. 34-40.

[Gadde,2001]

Gadde, S., Chase, J. and Rabinovich, M., "Web Caching and Content Distribution: A View from the Interior," *Computer Communication*, Vol. 24, No. 1-2, Jan. 2001, pp. 222-231.

[Gan,2000]

Gan, X. and Ramamurth, B., "LSMAC: An Improved Load Sharing Network Service Dispatcher," *World Wide Web*, Vol. 3, No. 1, Jan. 2000, pp. 53-59.

[Garcia,2003]

Garcia, D. and Garcia, J., "TPC-W e-Commerce Benchmark Evaluation," *IEEE Computer*, Vol. 36, No. 2, Feb. 2003, pp. 42-48.

[Garlan,D]

Garlon, D., Allen, R. and Ockerbloom, J. " Architectural Mismatch or Why it is Hard to Build Systems Out of Existing Parts," IEEE Software, Vol. 12, No.6, Nov. 1995, pp. 17-26.

[Ghini,2001]

Ghini, V., Panzieri, F. and Roccetti, M., "Client Centered Load Distributions: A Mechanism for Constructing Responsive Web Services," *Proceedings of the 34th Hawai International Conference on System Sciences (HICSS-34)*, Hawai, U.S.A, Jan.2001, Page 9020.

[Goswami,1993]

Goswami, K.K., Devarakonda, M. and Iyer, R.K., "Prediction Based Dynamic Load Sharing Heuristics," *IEEE Transactions on Parallel and Distributed System*, Vol. 4, No. 6, June 1992, pp. 638-648.

[Harchol-Balter,1997]

Harchol-Balter, M. and Downey, A.B., "Exploiting Process Lifetime Distributions for Dynamic Load Balancing," *ACM Transactions on Computer Systems*, Vol. 15, No. 3, Aug.1997, pp. 253-285.

[Harchol-Balter,1999]

Harchol-Balter, M. Crovella, M.E. and Murta, C., "Choosing a Task Assignment Policy for Distributed Server System," *Journal of Parallel and Distributed Computing*, 1999, pp. 204-228.

[Harchol-Balter,2003]

Harchol-Balter, M. et al., "Size Based Scheduling to Improve Web Performance," *ACM Transactions on Computer Systems*, Vol. 21, No.2, May 2003, pp. 207-233.

[Hendricson,2000]

Hendricson, B and Devine, K., "Dynamic Load Balancing in Computational Mechanics," Comp. Meth. Appl. in Mech. Engg., Vol. 184, 2000, pp. 485-500.

[Herbsleb,2003]

Herbsleb, J.D. and Mockus,, A. "An Empirical Study of Speed and Communication in Globally Distributed Software Development," *IEEE Transactions on Software Engineering*, Vol. 29, No. 6, June 2003, pp. 481-494.

[Hu,1998] Y.F., Blake, R.J. and Emerson, D.R., "An Optimal Migration Algorithm for Dynamic Load Balancing," *Concurrency: Practice and Experience*, Vol. 10, 1998, pp. 467-483.

[Hui,1999]

Hui, C.C. and Chandson, S.T., "Improved Strategies for Dynamic Load Balancing," *IEEE Concurrency*, Vol.7, No. 3, Jul.-Sept. 1999, pp. 58-67.

[Hunt,1998]

Hunt, G.S. et al., "Network Dispatcher: A Connection Router for Scalable Internet Services," *Computer Networks*, Vol. 30, No.1-7, 1998, pp. 347-357.

[Iyer,2000]

Iyer, R., Tewari and Kant K., "Overload Control Mechanisms for Web Servers," *Workshop on Performance and QoS of Next Generation Networks*, Nagoya, Japan, Nov. 2000.

[Jessica,2003]

Jessica, B. and Anthony, G.G., "Creating a Knowledge Sharing Community: If You Build It, Will They Come?" *ACM Communication*, Vol. 46, No. 2, Feb. 2003, pp. 23-25.

[Jiang,2004]

Jiang, H. and Choudhary, V., "Process Migration and Checkpoint in Heterogeneous Distributed Systems," *Proceedings of 37th Hawaii International Conference on System Sciences, (HICSS 04)*, Track 9, Page 90282b, 2004.

[Jinwan,2001]

Jinwan, H. and Tong, R., "Towards Optimal Resolution to Information Overload," *ACM, SIGROUP Conference on Supporting Workgroup*, Boulder, Colorado, USA, 30 Sept. to 3 Oct. 2001, pp. 91-96.

[Kanungo,2002]

Kanungo, P. and Vyas, N., "Dynamic Load Balancing in Distributed Systems," *International Conference on Knowledge Management(i-Maze)*, 21-22 Oct. 2002, IIPS, DAVV, Indore.

[Kanungo,2005]

Kanungo, P., "Performance Implications of Thread Management in Multiprocessor and Distributed Systems," *COMPUITNG-2005: CSI National Conference on Transferring Dreams into Reality,* 14-15 May 2005, Shri Vaishnav Institute of Technology and Science, Indore.

[Kanungo,2006a]

Kanungo, P. and Chandwani, M., "A Process Migration Methodology for Dynamic Load Balancing in Distributed Computing Environment," *Indian Journal of Computing Technology*, Vol. 1, No. 1, May 2006, pp. 11-21.

[Kanungo,2006b]

Kanungo, P. and Chandwani, M., "An Improved Dynamic Load Balancing Methodology for Distributed Computing Environment," *Communicated to Journal.*

[Kanungo,2006c]

Kanungo, P. and Chandwani, M., "Selection of Effective Load Indices Parameters and Performance Measurement in Dynamic Load Balancing Algorithms," *Communicated to Journal.*

[Kanungo,2006d]

Kanungo, P. and Chandwani, M., "Perfomance Implications of Dynamic Load Balancing in Networks and Web Servers," *Communicated to Journal.*

[Kanungo,2006e]

Kanungo, P. and Chandwani, M., "Recent Problems in Dynamic Load Balancing and Proposed Solutions," *Communicated to Journal.*

[Karatza,1997]

Karatza, H.D., "Simulation Study of Task Scheduling and Re-sequencing in a Multiprocessor System," *Simulation Journal, Special Issue: Modeling and Simulation of Computer Systems and Networks: Part Two, SCSI,* San Diego, CA, USA, Apr. 1997, pp. 241-247.

[Kartza,2000]

Kartza, H.D., "Scheduling Strategies for Multitasking in a Distributed System," *Proceedings of 33rd Annual Simulation System,* Washington D.C., USA, IEEE Computer Society, Los Alamitos, CA, USA, Apr. 2000, pp. 83-90.

[Kartza,2003]

Kartza, H.D., "A Comparative Analysis of Scheduling Policies in Distributed Systems Using Simulation," *International Journal of Simulation,* Vol. 1, No. 1-2, pp. 12-20.

[Kephart,2003]

Kephart, J.O. and Chess, D.M., "The Vision of Automatic Computing," *IEEE Computer Magazine,* Vol. 36, No. 1, 2003, pp. 41-50.

[Kwong,1999]

Kwong, P. and Majumdar, S., "Scheduling of I/O in Multiprogrammed Parallel Systems," *Informatica,* Vol.23, 1999, pp. 67-76.

[Lindermeier,2000]

Lindermeier, M., "Load Management for Distributed Object Oriented Environments," *Proceedings of the 2nd International Symposium on Distributed Objects and Applications (DOA 2000),* Antwerp, Belgium, Sept. 2000, OMG.

[Linux,2000]

Linux Virtual Server Project, http://www.linuxvirtualserver.org/

[Lu,1996]

Lu, C. and Lau, S., "An Adaptive Load Balancing Algorithm for Heterogeneous Distributed Systems with Multiple Task Classes," *Proceeding of 10th IEEE International Conference on Distributed Computing Systems (ICDSC-96),* 1996, pp. 629-636.

[Mcwherter,2004]

Mcwherter, D. et al., "Priority Based Mechanisms for OLTP and Transactional Web Applications," *20th International Conference on Data Engineering (ICDE 2004)*, Boston, MA, Apr. 2002, pp. 535-546.

[Menasce,2000]

Menasce, D.A. et al., "Business Oriented Resource Management Policies for e-Commerce Servers," *Performance Evaluation*, Vol. 42, No. 1-2, Sept. 2000, pp. 223-239.

[Milojicic,2000]

Milojicic, D.S. et al., "Process Migration," *ACM Computing Surveys*, pp. 241-299.

[Mitzenmacher,1997]

Mitzenmacher, M., "Analysis of Randomized Load Balancing Schemes," *Proceedings of 9th ACM Symposium on Parallel Algorithms and Architectures (SPAA '97)*, Newport, RI, June 1997, pp. 292-301.

[Mitzenmacher,2001]

Mitzenmacher, M. "The Power of Two Choices in Randomized Load Balancing," *IEEE Transactions on Parallel and Distributed Systems*, Vol. 12, No. 10, 2001, pp. 1094-1104.

[Mundie,2002]

Mundie, C., "Security: Source Access and the Software Ecosystem," *Conference on Open Source Software: Economics Law and Policy*, Toulouse, France, 20-21st June 2002.

[Nahum,2002]

Nahum, E.M., BARZILAI, T. and Kandulur, D.D., "Performance Issues in WWW Servers," *IEEE/ACM Transactions on Networking*, Vol. 10, No. 2, Feb. 2002, pp. 2-11.

[Newman,1997]

Newman, P., Minshall, G. and Huston, L., "IP Switching and Gigabit Routers," *IEEE Communications Magazine*, Vol. 35, No. 1., Jan. 1997, pp. 64-68.

[Nuttall,1994]

Nuttall, M., "A Brief Summary of Systems Providing Process or Object Migration Facilities," *ACM SIGOPS Operating System Review*, Vol. 28 No. 4, 1994, pp. 64-80.

[Othman,2003]

Othman, O. Balsubramanyam, J. and Schmidt, D., "The Design and Performance of an Adaptive Middleware Load Balancing and Monitoring Service," *Proceedings of Third International Workshop on Self Adaptive Software,* U.S.A., Arlington, VA, June2003.

[Otham,2001]

Otham, O., O'Ryan, C. and Schmidt, D., "Strategies for CORBA Middleware Based Load Balancing," *IEEE DS Online*, Vol. 2, No. 3, Mar. 2001.

[Pai,1998]

Pai, V.S. et al., "Locally Aware Request Distribution in Cluster Based Network Servers," *Proceedings of ACM 8th International Conference on Architectural Support for Programming Languages and Operating Systems (ASPLOSVIII)*, San Jose, CA, Oct. 1998, pp. 205-216.

[Pandey,1998]

Pandey, R., Barnes, J.F. and Olsson, R., "Supporting Quality of Service in HTTP Servers," *Proceedings of the ACM Symposium on Principles of Distributed Computing (Puerto Vallaria), Mexico,* ACM Press New York, June 1998, pp. 247-256.

[Petri,1995]

Petri, S. and Lingendorfer, H., "Load Balancing and Fault Tolerance in Workstation Clusters Migrating Groups of Communicating Processes," *ACM SIGOPS Operating Systems Review*, Vol. 29, No. 4, Oct. 1995, pp. 25-36.

[Pierre,2002]

Pierre, G., Van Steen, M. and Tanenbaum, A.S., "Dynamically Selecting Optimal Distribution Strategies for Web Documents," *IEEE Transactions on Computing*, Vol. 51, 2002, pp. 637-651.

[Phillips,1991]

Phillips, S., Yu, A. and Yann, H., "On Robust Transactions Routing and Load Sharing," *ACM Transactions on Database Systems,*" Vol. 16, No. 3, Sept. 1991, pp. 476-512.

[Powell,1983]

Powell, M.L. and Miller, B.F., "Process Migration in Demos/MP," *ACM*, 1983, pp. 110-119.

[Putrycz,2001]

Putrycz, E. and Bernard, G. "Client Side Reconfiguration on software component for Load Balancing," *IEEE Proceedings of ICDC2001 Workshop on Distributed Dynamic multi-service Architecture*, April 2001, Phoenix, USA, page 111.

[Putrycz,2002]

Putrycz, E., and Bernard, G., "Using Aspect Oriented Programming to Build a Portable Load Balancing Service," *IEEE Proceedings of the ICDS2002 International Conference on Distributed Computing Systems*, Vienna, Austria, July 2002, pp. 473-480.

[Qin,2004]

Qin, X. et al. "Dynamic Load Balancing for I/O Intensive Tasks on Heterogeneous Clusters," *Journal of Cluster Computing, Special Issue on Parallel I/O in Computational Grids and Cluster Computing Systems*, 2002.

[Richmond,1997]

Richmond, M. and Hitchens, M., "A New Process Migration Algorithm," *ACM SIGOPS Operating System Review*, Vol.31, No.1, 1997, pp. 31-40.

[Ridge,1997]

Ridge, D., Becker, D., Merkey, P. and Sterling, T., "Beowulf: Harnessing the Power of Parallelism in a Pile-of-PCs," *Proceedings of IEEE Aerospace, IEEE*, Vol. 2, 1997, pp. 79-91.

[Rosti,1998]

Rosti, E. et al., "The Impact of I/O, Program Behaviour and Parallel Scheduling," *Performance Evaluation Review, ACM*, New York, USA, Vol. 26, No.1, 1998, pp. 56-65.

[Rudolf,1991]

Rudolf, L., Slivkin-Allalouf, M. and Upfal, E, "A Simple Load Balancing Scheme for Task Allocation in Parallel Machines", *Proceedings of the Annual ACM Symposium on Parallel Algorithms and Architecture*, Hitron Head, South Carolina, U.S.A., July 1991 pp. 237-295.

[Sack,2003]

Sack, W. et al., "Social Architecture and Technological Determinism in Open Software Development," *International 4s Conference: Social Studies of Science and Society*, 2003, Atlanta, GA.

[Sarvotham,2001]

Sarvotham, S., Riedi, R. and Baraniuk., "R. Connection Level Analysis and Modeling of Network Traffic," *Proceeding of ACM SIGCOMM Internet Measurement Workshop*, San Francisco, CA, Nov. 2001, pp. 99-103.

[Scacchi,2001]

Scacchi, W. "Understanding the Requirements for Developing Open Source Software Systems," *IEEE Proceedings–Software*, Vol. 149, No. 1, 2001, pp. 24-39.

[Schagenhaft,1995]

Schagenhaft, R.M. et al., "Dynamic Load Balancing of a Multicluster Simulator on a Network of Workstations," *Proceeding of 9th Workshop on Parallel and Distributed Simulation (PADS 1995)*, pp.175-180.

[Selvam,2001]

Selvam, S., Moinuddin and Ibraheem, "Incorporation of Process Lifetime Distribution in Dynamic Load Balancing," *The Journal of Computer Society of India*, Vol. 31, No. 3, Sept. 2001, pp. 8-14.

[Sevcik,1994]

Sevcik, K., "Application Scheduling and Processor Allocation in Multiprogrammed and Parallel Processing Systems," *Performance Evaluation, Elsevier*, Amsterdam, Holland, Vol. 19, 1994, pp. 107-140.

[Shen,2002]

Shen, K., Yang T. and Chu L., "Cluster Load Balancing for Fine-Grain Network Services," *Technical Report TRCS2002-02*, Department of Computer Science, UC, Santa Barbara.

[Shaikh,1999]

Shaikh, A, Rexford, J. and Shin, K.G., "Load Sensitive Routing of Long Lived IP Flows," *ACM SIGCOMM Computer Communication Revolution*, Vol. 29, Oct. 1999, pp. 215-226.

[Shi,2005]

Shi, W., MacGreger, M.H. and Gburzynski, P., "Load Balancing for Parallel Forwarding," *IEEE/ACM Transactions on Networking*, Vol. 13, No. 4, Aug. 2005, pp. 790- 801.

[Shirazi,1995]

Shirazi, B.A., Hurson, A.R. and Kavi, K.M., Scheduling and Load Balancing in Parallel and Distributed Systems, *IEEE Computer Society Press*, Los Almitos, CA,1995.

[Singhal,1994]

Singhal, M. and Shivratri, N.G., Advance Concepts in Operating Systems, *McGraw Hill International Edition*, 1994.

[Sinha,2001]

Sinha, P. K., Distributed Operating Systems Concepts Design, *Prentice Hall of India*, 2001.

[Sloklic, 2002]

Sloklic, M. E., "Simulation of Load Balancing Algorithms: A Comparative Study," *SIGCSE Bulletin*, Vol. 34, No.4, Dec. 2002, pp. 138-141.

[Song,2002]

Song, J., Iyengar, A., Levy-Abegoli, E. and Dias, D., "Architecture of a Web Server Accelerator," *Computer Networks*, Vol. 38, No. 1, Jan. 2002, pp. 75-97.

[Stallings, 2003]

Stallings, W., *"Operating Systems"*, 4/e, Pearson Education, 2003.

[Stumm,1990]

Stumm, M. and Zhou, S., "Algorithms Implementing Distributed Shared Memory," *IEEE Computer*, Vol. 23, No. 5, 1990, pp. 54-64.

[Thitikamol,1999]

Thitikamol, K. and Kelehar, P., "Thread Migration and Communication minimization in DSM Systems," *Proceedings of IEEE*, Vol. 87, No. 3, March 1999, pp. 487-497.

[Tresco,2005]

Tresco, J.D., Faik, J. and Flaherty, F.E., "Resource Aware Scientific Computation on a Heterogeneous Cluster," *Computing in Science and Engineering*, Vol. 7, No. 2, 2005, pp. 40-50.

[Vallee,2002]

Vallee, G. et al., "Process Migration based on Gobelins Distributed Shared Memory," *Proceedings of 2nd IEEE/ACM International Symposium on Cluster Computing and Grid*, July 2002, pp.325- 330.

[Vutukury,1999]

Vutukury, S. and Garcia-Luna-Aceves, J.J., "A Simple Approximation to Minimum Delay Routing," *ACM SIGCOMM*, 1999, pp. 227-238.

[Waldspurger,1992]

Waldspurger et al., "Spawn: A Distributed Computational Economy," *IEEE Transactions on Software Engineering*, Vol.18, No.2, 1992.

[Wang,1993]

Wang, C., Krueger, P. and Liu, M.T., "Intelligent Job Selection for Distributed Scheduling," *Proceedings of 13th International Conference on Distributed Computing System*, May1993, pp. 517-524.

[Wang,1999]

Wang, J., "A Survey of Web Caching Schemes for the Internet," *ACM Computer Communication Review*, Vol. 25, No. 9, Oct. 1999, pp. 36-46.

[Watts,1998a]

Watts, J., Rieffel, M. and Taylor, S., "Dynamic Management of Heterogeneous Resources," *High Performance Computing Conference: Grand Challenges in Computer Simulations,* April 1998, pp. 151-156.

[Watts,1998b]

Watts, J. and F., Taylor A., "Practical Approach to Dynamic Load Balancing," *IEEE Transactions on Parallel and Distributed Systems*, Vol. 9, No.3, 1998, pp. 235-248.

[Welsh,2003]

Welsh, M. and Culler, D., "Adaptive Overload Management for Busy Internet Servers," *Proceedings of the 4th USENIX Symposium on Internet Technologies and Systems (USITS '03)*, Seattle, WA, Mar. 2003.

[Willebeek,1993]

Willebeek, M. et al., "Strategies for Dynamic Load Balancing on Highly Parallel Computers," *IEEE Parallel and Distributed Systems*, Vol. 4, No. 9, 1993, pp. 979-993.

[Wilson,1998]

Wilson, L.F. and Shen, W., "Experiments in Load Migration and Dynamic Load Balancing in SPEEDS," *Proceedings of Winter Simulation Conference*, 1998, pp. 483-490.

[Williams,2002]

Williams, S., "Free as in Freedom-Richard Stallman's Crusade for Free Software," O'Reilly, Available at http://www.oreilly.com/openbook/freedom.

[Wolf,2001]

Wolf, J.L. and Yu, P.S., "On Balancing the Load in a Cluster Web Farm," *ACM Transactions on Internet Technology,* 1-2, Nov. 2001, pp. 231-251.

[Xiao,2000]

Xiao., L., Zhand, Z. and Qu, Y., "Effective Load Sharing on Heterogeneous Network of Work Stations," *IEEE Proceedings IDDDS'2000*, Cancun, 8 pages.

[Xu,1993]

Xu, J. and Hwang, K., "Heuristic Methods for Dynamic Load Balancing in a Message Passing Multicomputer," *Journal of Parallel and Distributed Computing*, Vol. 18, No.1, May 1993, pp. 888-897.

[Yagoubi,2005]

Yagoubi, B., "Dynamic Load balancing for Beowulf Cluster," *Proceedings of the International Arab Conference on Information Technology*, Israa University, Jardon, 6-8 Dec. 2005, pp. 394-401.

[Yagoubi,2006]

Yagoubi, B. and Slimani, Y., "Dynamic Load Balancing Strategy for Grid Computing," *Enformatica Transactions on Engineering Computing and Technology*, Vol. 13, 2006, pp. 260-265.

[Yang,2000]

Yang, C.S. and Luo, M.Y., "A Content Placement and Management system for Distributed Web Server Systems," *Proceedings of the 20th IEEE International Conference on Distributed Computing Systems*, Taipei, Taiwan, April 2000, pp. 691-698.

[Zaki,1997]

Zaki, M.J., Wei, L. and Parthsarthy, S., "Customized Dynamic Load Balancing for a Network of Workstations," *Journal of Parallel and Distributed Computing,* Vol. 43, 1997, pp. 156-162.

[Zhang,2005]

Zhang, K. and Pande, S., "Efficient Application Migration under Compiler Guidance," *Proceedings of 2005 ACM SIGPLAN/SIGBED Conference on Language, Compilers and Tools of Embedded Systems (LCTES, 2005)*, Chicago, Illinois, U.S.A., pp. 11-20.

[Zhang,1999]

Zhang, X. et al., "An Architecture for Cluster Based Web Servers," *Proceedings of 3rd USENIX Windows NT Symposium*, Seattle, WA, July 1999, pp. 155-164.

[Zhang,2002]

Zhang, Q. et al., "Workload Aware Load Balancing for Cluster Web Servers," *22nd International Conference on Distributed Computer Systems, (ICDCS '02)*, Vienna, Austria, July 2002, pp. 103-111.

[Zhong,1997]

Zhong, Y. Kameda, H. and Hung, S.L., "Comparison of Dynamic and Static Load Balancing Strategies in Distributed Systems," *IEEE Proceedings of Computer and Digital Techniques*, Vol. 144, No. 2, Mar. 1997.

[Zhou,1988]

Zhou, S., "A Trace Driven Simulation Study of Dynamic Load Balancing," *IEEE Transactions on Software Engineering*, Vol. 14, No. 9, Sept. 1988, pp. 1327-1341.

[Zhu,1999]

Zhu, H., Smith, B. and Yang, T., "Scheduling Optimization for Resource Intensive Web Requests on Server Clusters," *Proceedings of the 11th ACM Symposium on Parallel Algorithms and Architectures (SPAA'99)*, Saint Malo, France, June 1999, pp. 13-22.

[Zhu,2001]

Zhu, H., Tang, H. and Yang, T., "Demand Driven Service Differentiation in Cluster Based Network Servers," *Proceedings of the 20th IEEE International Conference on Computer Communications (INFOCOM 2001)*, Anchorage, AK, Apr. 2001, pp. 679-688.

[Zhu,1997]

Zhu, W., Sacko, P. and Kiepuszewski, B., "Migration Impact on Load Balancing: An Experience on Amoeba," *ACM SIGOPS Operating System Review*, Vol. 31, No.1, 1997, pp. 45-53.

ABOUT THE AUTHOR

Dr Priyesh Kanungo is working as a Professor and Senior Systems Engineer in Computer Centre at the School of Computer Science and Information Technology, Devi Ahilya Vishwavidyalaya (DAVV), Indore.

He received a B.E. (Industrial and Production Engg.), M.E. (Computer Engineering) from SGSITS, Indore and M Phil and a **Ph D. in Computer Engineering**.

He has more than 26 years of teaching experience in M Tech, Ph D, M.C.A., M.B.A., B.E. etc. in DAVV, Indore. He has been teaching various subjects like Operating Systems, Systems Programming, Data Structures, DBMS and AI.

Areas of research of Dr Priyesh Kanungo are **Advance Operating Systems, Distributed Computing, Grid Computing and Cloud Computing**. He has guided a number of Ph Ds and is presently guiding eight students. He has published around 50 research papers in reputed international journals and conferences (including IEEE, ACM and Springer). He also is an UGC expert for Computer Science, Applications and Engineering.